MAYOR
KANE

MAYOR
KANE

MY LIFE IN WRESTLING
AND POLITICS

GLENN JACOBS

CENTER
STREET

New York Nashville

Center Street
Hachette Book Group
1290 Avenue of the Americas, New York, NY 10104
centerstreet.com
twitter.com/centerstreet

First Edition: November 2019

Center Street is a division of Hachette Book Group, Inc. The Center Street name and logo are trademarks of Hachette Book Group, Inc.

The publisher is not responsible for websites (or their content) that are not owned by the publisher.

The Hachette Speakers Bureau provides a wide range of authors for speaking events. To find out more, go to www.HachetteSpeakersBureau.com or call (866) 376-6591.

Library of Congress Cataloging-in-Publication Data has been applied for

ISBNs: 978-1-5460-8584-3 (hardcover), 978-1-5460-8537-9 (signed edition), 978-1-5460-8536-2 (BN.com signed edition), 978-1-5460-8582-9 (ebook)

Printed in the United States of America

LSC-C

10 9 8 7 6 5 4 3 2 1

CONTENTS

CONTENTS

FOREWORD BY UNDERTAKER

It's hard to imagine a performer for WWE who has been more integral to the popularity and evolution of Undertaker than Kane has been for over twenty years.

It's also hard to imagine a better person in the pro wrestling business than Kane, aka Glenn Jacobs, who performed as my half brother for many years.

When Glenn entered the ring as Kane in 1997, many observers thought his career as a wrestler for WWE might be brief. The conventional wisdom was that I would work with him for a short period of time before moving on to other opponents. If you had asked Glenn back then, he likely would have told you the same thing.

That's, obviously, not what happened. Kane became a force in his own right, headlining the biggest shows during the height of WWE's popularity in the 1990s. Having Kane, Stone Cold Steve Austin, The Rock (aka Dwayne Johnson), Mankind (aka Mick Foley), Triple H, and Undertaker all in the main-event mix during the Attitude Era. That was the time, from 1997 to 1999, when WWE's *Monday Night Raw* went head-to-head with World Championship Wrestling's *Monday Nitro*, and it is a time I will never forget. That was like the Mount Rushmore of wrestling, with all of the legends on top at once.

Nor will I ever forget all the great times Glenn and I had with the late, great Paul Bearer.

Kane accomplished so much separate from his work with Undertaker. From becoming World Champion multiple times to teaming with Daniel Bryan to form Team Hell No, and even going corporate to join The Authority, he has seen and done it all in WWE, constantly reinventing himself to repeated success.

Still, whenever Kane and I, Undertaker, teamed up as The Brothers of Destruction, no one could touch us. We were unstoppable.

During the many years I've known Glenn, he has always been one of the smartest guys in the locker room. So, I wasn't surprised when, in 2018, he was elected mayor of Knox County, Tennessee. I know how much he and his family love their home there and how passionate he is about politics and helping his friends and neighbors.

Glenn might be the nicest person in WWE, which is an accomplishment for anyone who has been in our business since 1992, when he made his wrestling debut. I'm sure Glenn will find politics just as challenging, but I know it won't change him. He is considerate and truly cares about others. The Glenn you see is the Glenn you get.

Every day, both of us appreciate the unique lives we've lived in WWE. The stories we've told in the ring will remain etched in the minds of many long after we're gone. That's quite a legacy.

For Kane and Undertaker, I wouldn't change a thing that's happened over the last two decades. Demon and Deadman's inseparable journey has been an incredible one; you just never know where The Brothers of Destruction might pop up next.

FOREWORD
BY SEN. RAND PAUL
(R-KY)

My friend Glenn Jacobs has not only made a name for himself in the WWE world, but has been politically active and community oriented for years, doing everything he can to serve his neighbors at home in Tennessee. When he was elected mayor in 2018, I knew not only that the people of Knox County had chosen a quality leader who would work hard for them, but a genuinely decent person who is involved in politics for all the right reasons.

That's hard to find in Washington or anywhere else.

I first met Glenn in New Hampshire in 2007. He was hard to miss. Standing head and shoulders above the crowd that had gathered to support my father's presidential campaign, Glenn's sheer size immediately captured one's attention.

Like so many young people from disparate backgrounds, Glenn was a part of the "Ron Paul Revolution," a movement focused on injecting libertarian and constitutionalist ideas back into a GOP where they had been missing or dormant for years.

When I returned home to Kentucky from New Hampshire, many friends wanted to know if I had met other GOP candidates, like former Massachusetts governor Mitt Romney or Sen. John McCain of Arizona, but my kids were more interested to learn that I had met Kane. My middle son insisted on me getting him a Kane poster, and we went to see him wrestle in Diddle Arena at Western Kentucky University in Bowling Green.

Over the years, I came to know Kane as Glenn and to appreciate his academic and intellectual talents, which go beyond his feats of brawn.

In 2010, when I ran for an open U.S. Senate seat in Kentucky, I appreciated Glenn's support, and the feeling has always been mutual. Eight years later, in 2018, I had the privilege of supporting him in his run for mayor.

It was an easy endorsement to make. I don't often get involved in state or city races because, frankly, few in my party understand that less government and more liberty are key if Americans are going to achieve their dreams. Many mouth the rhetoric because they think they're supposed to, but few follow through and take it seriously. Glenn actually gets it. He's thought about these ideas and about his own political philosophy in a deeper way than most.

Glenn and I also both ran as outsiders. I had never held public office before running for U.S. Senate. I was, and still am, an ophthalmologist by trade. Glenn had never held public office before becoming mayor of Knox County. He had traveled the world as an internationally known WWE star for decades, something some career politicians might have tried to use against him.

But the old rules don't apply anymore. People are tired of the same old politics. They want more outsiders getting involved in politics. Americans across the board are tired of the status quo.

Just ask the current occupant of the White House. Glenn didn't need to become mayor. He wanted to because of his passion and commitment to public service. The fact that he's not a lifelong politician is an asset, not a liability. It's a big part of what makes him such a good mayor. Glenn's pro-liberty and small-government philosophy on virtually everything—education, the economy, regulation, taxes, property rights, free markets, individual freedoms, you name it—is exactly what we need more of in this country. We also need it at every level—federal, state, and local—maximizing freedom and minimizing government wherever possible.

Most Republicans at any level will agree, in theory, that we need a greater amount of fiscal responsibility and fewer politicians trying to run our lives. But nine times out of ten, Republicans are just as much a part of the problem as anyone else. Believe me, I'm surrounded by them in Washington every day.

Very few are serious about the ideas of liberty. Glenn Jacobs is one of those few.

MAYOR
KANE

PROLOGUE

In October 2018, I boarded a private charter jet at McGhee Tyson Airport, just south of Knoxville, bound for Seattle. The previous month, I had assumed office as the mayor of Knox County, Tennessee. But that night I would make a surprise appearance on *Monday Night Raw*, where Undertaker and I would close the show by Chokeslamming Shawn Michaels and Triple H.

The crowd went absolutely bonkers.

I would return home in the same private jet, arriving at 4 a.m. the following day to prepare for a mayoral press conference about an important lawsuit concerning Knox County. WWE had hired the jet so that I could make it back home in time for my day job.

Just your typical day at the office, right?

As I sat waiting on the plane, I had to smile. I even shook my head, amazed at the whole situation.

What life was this? Who am I? How did I get so lucky?

How in the world did I get here?

Thirty years before, in 1988, I was an injured football

player, worried about what I was going to do with the rest of my life. For a time, I was genuinely clueless—scared, even—about what might come next. Such is the case for many young people starting out.

Yet here I was, a globally known Superstar for the biggest pro wrestling company on the planet, WWE, and I had also just become mayor of the third-largest county in the state, with nearly half a million residents!

On paper, all of this seemed completely insane!

Anyone would have felt blessed to have just one of these jobs. Yet here I was doing both of them—on the *same day*.

And they go hand in hand. For over two decades, WWE has given me a global platform to entertain and make people happy. The resulting fame, in turn, has allowed me to pursue my passion for freedom and liberty, and working to make my home of Knox County, Tennessee, a better place.

Kane has always been an outcast or a loner. Someone who walks to the beat of his own drum. Similarly, Glenn Jacobs, the man, became mayor precisely because I'm not a politician. I'm different. From the moment I stepped into the political arena, I was looked at with skepticism and curiosity by nearly all the professional politicians and so-called experts.

Few thought back in 1997 that Kane, the brother of Undertaker, was a character that would stick around for long, but here I was still going strong after twenty-plus years.

Few thought that a nearly seven-foot-tall WWE Superstar could ever be taken seriously as a political candidate, and yet

I shocked my county, my state, and the world by winning my race for mayor!

Few would have ever thought.

But I had learned a long time before then that what other people think about you isn't nearly as important as what you believe about yourself.

CHAPTER I

RAISING KANE

When I was eight years old and living on our family's small farm in northeastern Missouri, Baron von Raschke scared me so badly that I turned off the TV.

Once a month, my family would travel to my grandmother's house outside St. Louis. The highlight of the trip was sitting cross-legged in front of Grandma's TV on Saturday morning and watching *Wrestling at the Chase*, which was then one of the country's premier professional wrestling shows.

Wrestling at the Chase featured some of the biggest stars in the sport, including Harley Race, Ric Flair, and the Von Erich family. But it was von Raschke, a villainous German whose bald head and snarling demeanor bore a passing resemblance to Freddy Krueger, who made an indelible imprint on my young psyche.

Little did I know then that professional wrestling, which would evolve into what we know today as "sports entertainment," would play such an integral role in my life. And, like von Raschke, I would find most of my success as a vicious heel who scared people half to death!

Hailing from Madrid, Spain

April 26, 1967, was an uneventful day in the history of Torrejón Air Base in Madrid, Spain. But it was a momentous day for me as U.S. Air Force master sergeant George Jacobs and his wife, Joan, welcomed their bouncing baby boy, Glenn Thomas Jacobs, into the world.

My mom and dad had both grown up in West Alton, Missouri, a small town of a few hundred people right outside St. Louis. While I have some English and Dutch ancestors, I come from mostly German stock. In fact, my mother's maiden name is Reichmann. Before moving to America, it was pronounced "Rike-mon," about as German sounding as you can get. After coming to the United States, the family Americanized it to "Reek-mon."

My mother's family farmed in the Missouri Bottoms area of the Mississippi River floodplain, some of the most fertile soil in the country. My dad's father was a carpenter and a veteran of World War I who was awarded a Purple Heart and a Silver Star fighting on the Western Front.

Mom and Dad got married shortly after high school. By this time, Dad had already enlisted in the Navy. He served in the Navy for ten years, seeing action during the Korean War on the aircraft carrier USS *Antietam*. He later switched services to the Air Force.

His eleven years in the USAF included a stint in Vietnam. As a loadmaster, Dad was in charge of weight and balance calculations on the big planes, like the Air Force's gigantic Lockheed C-130 Hercules, which was designed to transport troops and cargo. He gave the approval for a flight to take off, one of the rare instances where an enlisted man could overrule a general.

Upon entering the world, I joined my sister, Becky, who was then ten, and my brother, Bryan, eight. I've often wondered why I came so long after my siblings, and if I was an unexpected accident or a pleasant surprise—or both.

My father is on record as saying that I was the only planned baby, but I think he says that just to make me feel better!

Becky, Bryan, and Me

Other than being tall and kind of looking alike, Becky, Bryan, and I are about as diverse as you can be. Becky definitely got the brains in the family. She worked for a while at NASA, then earned her PhD in history. Today, she is a professor at a community college in Oklahoma. Bryan is a gifted mechanic. For as long as I can remember, he has been taking apart, fixing, and putting back together anything that has moving parts.

I was the family athlete, although it took a while for my talents to manifest.

Unlike Becky and Bryan, I never experienced the military lifestyle—moving around every year or so—that many kids do. About a year after I was born, we came back to the United States; three years later, Dad retired from the Air Force.

We settled on a small farm about a twenty-minute drive from the town of Bowling Green, in northeastern Missouri. We lived about a mile from a little unincorporated hamlet called Estes.

You've probably heard about towns that have only one stoplight. Estes had just one stop *sign*. The main attraction in Estes—in fact, the only attraction—was the general store.

Occasionally, I would walk down the country highway with Becky or Bryan to get a Coke and listen and watch as the old-timers chewed the fat...and, of course, tobacco. The sodas cost a nickel each, and you opened them with the bottle opener screwed into the side of an ice-filled metal box, which acted as the cooler.

On a hot Missouri summer day, those ice-cold Coca-Colas were almost as good as the signature lemon meringue pies at the Presbyterian church's ladies auxiliary club's bake sales!

I clearly had my priorities straight as a kid.

In the middle of our little farm sat a boulder, which became the source of a family controversy. This rock—a large, reddish hunk about three feet around, nestled peacefully in a meadow—was completely out of place and inconsistent with the rest of the geology of the place.

Mom claimed that it was a meteorite and wanted to send a sample to the University of Missouri so that geologists there could examine it. Looking back now, it's obvious that a meteorite that size would have created a massive crater. But, at the time, the idea of an extraterrestrial object in our backyard was exciting to me, which may explain my later, fleeting fascination with UFOs and all things outer space.

Growing up on a farm was not really the bucolic, romanticized life that you read about in novels. For instance, consider the smells.

They're not exactly fragrant.

Across the road from our house was a large hog farm. When the wind blew the right way, we relaxed on the porch, and enjoyed the pleasant evenings. But when the breeze shifted, which it often did within a couple of minutes, the clean country air was replaced by the stench of manure from hundreds of hogs.

The WCW pay-per-view *Hog Wild* was sweet and genteel compared to our swine experience!

On our farm, we raised a few cattle and some hogs. One of my earliest memories was waking early in the morning to accompany Dad to the barn. One of our sows had given birth to a litter of piglets. Dad was making sure that she didn't roll over on them and accidentally kill them.

Another time, we discovered a bloated cow in our cornfield. She had fallen onto her side and couldn't get back up. I watched in fascination and horror as my parents inserted a corkscrew-shaped trocar between the poor beast's ribs to relieve the pent-up gas.

I was completely mortified. Fortunately the cow survived and was soon back to normal. As for me, well, there are some things you just can't unsee.

By the time I was in third grade, Becky and Bryan had both moved out of the house. Becky had graduated high school and was attending the University of Missouri at Columbia. She stayed there only a year, though. Mizzou was a big school and too impersonal for her. She ended up being accepted into a work-study program at NASA's Johnson Space Center and moved to Houston, where she attended the University of Houston–Clear Lake. Eventually, she would earn a bachelor's degree in mathematics. Then another undergraduate degree in archeology. Then a PhD in history.

To say she's accomplished is an understatement.

Bryan had gone to live with Grandma near St. Louis so that he could attend a vocational school and study auto mechanics. He was always so good with his hands. A natural talent.

From something as small as a watch to a piece of heavy machinery, Bryan can fix it.

I couldn't have asked for a better brother and sister.

Baseball, Basketball, and Hulk Hogan

After Becky and Bryan left home, I essentially became an only child. Granted, because of our age differences, it wasn't like we had been playmates. But I enjoyed their company, especially Becky's.

I remember a Halloween party Becky hosted at our house for some of her friends. At the time, the movie *Billy Jack* was a hit. We will never again see so many barefooted teenagers wearing flat-brimmed, round-domed cowboy hats in one place as were at our house that night!

Growing up alone had its advantages. I think that it really helped enrich my imagination.

My parents were always big readers, and I would often immerse myself in books to pass the time. My favorites were Westerns by Louis L'Amour. I also learned that I was pretty good company and felt comfortable in my own skin.

Despite having pursued careers that have placed me in the public eye, I am very much an introvert and would rather read a book at home than socialize out on the town. I'm convinced that my childhood has a lot to do with that.

Around my fourth-grade year, my family moved about an hour away to another small farm, near a town of about three hundred residents called Frankford. Halloween night in Frankford was reminiscent of Devil's Night in the movie *The Crow*. For years, unruly folks dragged junk cars to the middle of Main Street and set them on fire!

Luckily that was the most exciting thing to happen in town, except possibly when Frankford native P. J. Lansing appeared as *Playboy* magazine's Playmate of the Month in its February 1972 issue. Nevertheless, if Lansing's centerfold had caused any buzz in Frankford, it had long since dissipated by the time we arrived about five years later.

Since I was new at school, I certainly wasn't the most popular kid. Add to that my height, and my social and physical awkwardness, and I often felt that I didn't fit in. I was a naturally good student. Not great, but good.

From an early age, I was passionate about sports, especially baseball. Growing up near St. Louis, I was a huge Cardinals fan. I fondly remember staying up late during the summer to listen as KMOX's legendary radio duo of Jack Buck and Mike Shannon called a Cardinals West Coast road trip.

My dream was to play for the Cardinals. I recall setting up an imaginary scenario in which it was the bottom of the ninth inning in the World Series. The Cardinals were down by three runs, and the bases were loaded with two outs. With the image firmly in mind, I toss a rock into the air and swing at it with a stick.

Unfortunately, I was a pretty horrible baseball player. I didn't hit that rock very often. I don't think I even had a hit in my entire Little League baseball career.

Because of my height, I was a much better basketball player. But until my body matured, my dreams of playing professional sports were just that—dreams! I kept trying, though, playing football and basketball in middle school. By eighth grade, I was six feet, four inches tall and still growing. Knowing my brother, Bryan, was close to six foot eight, I figured basketball was my best bet and I decided to concentrate on that.

I was a pretty good basketball player, and I kept getting better as I grew into my body. By the time I was a senior in high school, I was being recruited by a number of colleges, including some Division 1 schools. I had also become a pretty decent student by that time, graduating in 1985 from Bowling Green High School, the county's consolidated high school, in the top 10 percent of my class.

I am totally proud to be a child of the '80s. My teenage years were dominated by Arnold Schwarzenegger, Michael

J. Fox, early home video game systems like the Atari 2600, iconic "feuds" like the one between Larry Bird and Magic Johnson, and TV shows like *The Dukes of Hazzard* and *The A-Team*.

But most of all, I was smitten by music videos on MTV. Like millions of other teenagers, I'd race home or to a friend's house after school to watch the latest videos on the relatively new cable music channel.

And I wasn't the only one who took note of the rise of MTV. Much of the success of WWE in the 1980s can be traced to the decision by WWE Chairman and CEO Vince McMahon to partner with and promote artists like Cyndi Lauper.

And, just as MTV was changing entertainment, a blond, bulging behemoth named Hulk Hogan was changing professional wrestling.

Tanned and muscular, Hogan looked nothing like the pro wrestlers I remembered from my childhood. He was a superhero come to life. I'll never forget watching Hogan slam Andre the Giant at *WrestleMania III*. I'd injured my ankle playing basketball and was in a hospital bed when the clip played on the syndicated show *The George Michael Sports Machine*.

Nevertheless, my interest in pro wrestling was still just as a casual fan. I'd earned a basketball scholarship to attend Quincy College (now Quincy University) in Illinois, about an hour's drive north of Frankford.

After a year and a half there, I became frustrated with my role on the team and transferred to Northeast Missouri State University (NEMO) in Kirksville, less than two hours from Frankford.

Like many young people, I wasn't sure what I wanted to do with my life. I'd started my college career as a computer science major, but I just wasn't that adept at it. Thinking that I might like to teach, I switched my major to English.

At NEMO, they were introducing a program for education majors and I got caught in the transition. So, while I would eventually earn a BA in English, I would graduate a couple of hours short of my teaching certification.

When I graduated high school, I only weighed about 230 pounds. That's pretty slim on a six-eight frame. I'd only played basketball and had never really lifted weights.

All that changed when I began college.

"I'll Be Practicing with the Chicago Bears!"

I spent the summer between my senior year in high school and my freshman year in college with Becky in Houston, where I joined the local Gold's Gym. Over the following couple of months, I put on twenty pounds of muscle.

In college, my coaches encouraged me to lift and I loved it! Lifting weights became one of my main pastimes; by senior year, I weighed about 285 pounds.

Talk about large and in charge!

By then, I had played four years of basketball. But as I bulked up, the football coach began talking to me more and more about joining his team, something I had never considered before. I had one year of eligibility left if I decided to switch from basketball to football. With a few hours left to get my degree and my only prospects of playing basketball professionally in question, I decided: What the heck!

I donned a helmet and pads.

I discovered that my body was made for football. As I continued to lift weights (and eat *a lot*), I eventually tipped the scales at 320 pounds!

Playing basketball all those years had helped me retain my athleticism. Being a Division 2 school, we rarely had NFL scouts watching our practices, but they showed up to watch me.

I was receiving letters of interest from the Dallas Cowboys and other NFL teams. ESPN's NFL draft analyst Mel Kiper Jr. had a list of potential picks to move up to the pros, and I was ranked at number 25.

I hadn't played football since the eighth grade!

But, as often happens, life had different plans for me. It was the first practice of our first game week of the season. Practice was essentially over. Given the day's high heat index, we weren't running sprints or doing any conditioning. By now, the team had the playbook down pat, so the last fifteen minutes of practice was devoted to going through some trick plays.

We were walking through the plays at three-quarters speed, no contact, and had removed our helmets and shoulder pads. This particular play was a wide receiver reverse.

I was playing right offensive tackle and the play was coming to my side. The quarterback would fake a handoff to the running back on a play to the opposite side and then make the handoff to a wideout who was running my way. My job was to allow the opposing defensive end or outside linebacker to get around me, then—as he realizes his mistake and turns to pursue the wide receiver—clean his clock.

The center hiked the ball and the play began to develop. I allowed the linebacker to get past me, but as I pivoted a strange thing happened. Somehow, I was on my back on the ground.

Seriously, I had no idea what had happened. One second I was on my feet. The next I was on my back.

No one had hit me. I just fell.

Then, as I got back up to my feet, my left knee buckled and I fell again. This time, when I tried to get up, I couldn't put any weight on that knee. There was no pain. The knee just wasn't stable enough to hold me upright.

By now, the whole team had gathered around to see what was up. Finally, the training staff came over to look at me. After discovering that moving my knee in a couple of different directions caused some discomfort, they helped me off the field and into the training room.

I got undressed and they wrapped ice on my knee. I showered, took the ice off, and went home on crutches with my knee in a splint. By now, the knee had become tender and was beginning to swell.

When I woke up the next day, my left knee was howling with pain and continuing to swell. Our head trainer, Clint Thompson (who, incidentally, was the head trainer at Michigan State University the year they won a national championship with Magic Johnson), thought that I had torn my anterior cruciate ligament (ACL).

My parents drove to Kirksville, picked me up, and took me to the University of Missouri at Columbia for an exploratory arthroscopic procedure. The surgery confirmed Clint's diagnosis. I had suffered a partial tear of my ACL and damaged the meniscus in my left knee.

Since I didn't have the medical hardship waiver called a medical redshirt, I had no choice but to play that season or end my career without having played a single college game. So I worked very hard at rehab and was back on the field after six weeks.

Unfortunately, I just wasn't the player that I had been before the injury. I didn't have the explosiveness or the agility that I had possessed previously. I also guarded my knee. For an offensive lineman, it's all about footwork. Depending on which way the play is going, you have to take certain steps in a certain way. If you don't, you will never make the play.

After the injury, I had a lot of trouble leading with my left foot. Often, it was an unconscious fear. I was gun-shy about using that leg.

Despite my struggles, the team had an excellent year. We ended up with a 9-2 record, losing in the national Division 2 playoffs. Of course, I didn't contribute much, if at all, to that success, but it was a memorable season nonetheless.

Though I still didn't give up on my dream, my prospects appeared much dimmer now.

I graduated in the winter semester of 1990 and moved back home. I got a job working in a group home for individuals with special needs. But I kept training hard, hoping that I could get a shot in the NFL.

I wasn't invited to the NFL Scouting Combine, the annual weeklong showcase in Indianapolis for college athletes, but I did work out with a couple of teams. When draft day came, I was pretty excited. My agent told me that a few teams were willing to take a chance on me and I could expect to be drafted in the later rounds.

That didn't happen. I can't say that I was shocked by this turn of events. After all, here I was, a basketball player turned football player who had minimal experience playing at a small school and had suffered a severe knee injury less than a year before. Not exactly a recipe for success as an NFL prospect.

However, I was elated when, a few days later, my agent told me that the Chicago Bears had offered me a contract as an undrafted free agent. It even included a $5,000 signing bonus!

A couple of weeks later, I flew from Lambert International Airport in St. Louis to Chicago O'Hare International Airport, where a car picked me up and whisked me off to the Bears' training facility in Lake Forest, Illinois. There, all the rookies went through a battery of physicals, everything from vision tests to hearing tests to, of course, orthopedic tests.

At the end of the day, we met with our position coaches who told us what to expect the next day at the minicamp. I went to bed that night on cloud nine. "Tomorrow," I thought, "I'll be practicing with the Chicago Bears!"

The next morning, a bus carried the rookies who were staying in the hotel to the Bears' training facility.

Then, a funny thing happened.

While all the other potential Bears exited the bus and headed over to the fieldhouse, a Bears representative escorted another player and me to a nearby office building. We were ushered into the office of the director of player personnel, where we were informed that each of us had an injury that precluded us from playing for the Chicago Bears.

"Sorry, guys," he told us in a sympathetic voice, "we just can't take a chance on you." From there, a car took me back to the airport and I caught a flight home. The whole experience had lasted just over twenty-four hours.

I was devastated.

Coming back from an injury like the one I had suffered had been no small feat. Rehab had been physically painful and emotionally draining. Many times throughout the process I had wanted to give up. So often it felt too hard and not worth it. Time and again, I had talked myself off the figurative ledge and told myself I could make it through another day; that it was worth it; that I owed it to myself to give it my best. Clichés, I know, but still true.

In the end, all that work and effort had been a waste. At least, that was what I told myself. For a couple of weeks, I wallowed in self-pity. Looking back, I'm pretty ashamed of that.

At the same time, I was still a kid and my life's dream had been viciously snatched away from me just when it seemed like I was on the verge of fulfilling it.

Finally, I decided that I needed to get on with my life. There was still a slim chance that I could end up in the NFL via the newly formed World League of American Football, the NFL's nascent minor league. So, I got back into the gym and started training again the only way that I knew how: hard and heavy.

I've heard it said that, in life, when one door closes, another one opens. That's not exactly what happens, though. It's not nearly that sanitary or peaceful. The door slams violently just when you are about to step through. It knocks you down, leaves you bloodied and broken and shattered. Sometimes, the hardest thing that you will ever do is pick up the pieces and haul yourself back up on your feet.

But when you do, you realize that these other doors have been there all along; you just never saw them before. They don't just pop open. You've got to force them open through determination and hard work.

Deep down, I knew that my chances of playing in the NFL were as good as dead. But I also knew that there were only a few individuals on the planet who were as tall and muscular as I was; who were as physically impressive and imposing as I was; who possessed the innate athleticism that I had for someone my size.

It all clicked one evening when I was watching *WWE Prime Time Wrestling* with my buddy Mark Morton at his house in nearby Louisiana, Missouri. Mark, a huge WWE fan, joked that he and I should give professional wrestling a try.

In my mind, I suddenly saw a door that I'd never considered before. The question was: How would I open it?

CHAPTER 2

GET IN THE RING

Born in a Barn

"Ker-smack!" My forearm crashed down onto Mark's back with a thunderous slap.

"Man, you're killing him," said my trainer, T.C. Rocannon, aka "Nightmaster." I couldn't get it through my head that T.C. was telling me to pause with my hand raised over my head for dramatic effect before I unleashed the blow.

I thought he meant I should just hit Mark harder! Luckily, Mark was a good sport...plus, I probably owed him a few anyway!

My career in sports entertainment started from very humble beginnings. In fact, these first lessons were actually in a ring that T.C. had set up in the hayloft over his barn!

Once a week, Mark and I would make the hour-long trip to T.C.'s farm close to Kingdom City, Missouri. There, we learned some rudimentary skills, like how to "take a bump," which is wrestling parlance for getting knocked to the mat in a way that looks violent but causes the body the least amount of harm. We also learned how to give and take moves, and pantomime punches, kicks, and other strikes. We also talked a little about how to develop a persona.

Mark and I had been directed to T.C. after attending a small, independent wrestling show. There, we saw local stars like The Shadow Warriors, Matt Michaels, and Lunatic Maxx. The featured match was an over-the-top-rope battle royal. I was mesmerized as I watched the participants fly over the top rope and hit the ground with a sickening slap.

How did that not kill these guys? After the show, we spoke with the promoter, Frank Root. Frank gave us T.C.'s number and told us to call him.

The training wasn't free. T.C. charged each of us $50 per lesson. At the time, I was working at the group home for people with special needs, and that was a pretty hefty sum for me, but I was hooked and figured that I might have a future in this business.

After a few months, I had my first match. It was in front of around three hundred people in the ballroom of the Stegton Regency Banquet Center in St. Charles, Missouri, just outside St. Louis.

I wore tights that my mom had made for me!

I'd always thought the name "Angus" was cool, so I assumed the ring moniker Angus King from Glasgow, Scotland. My opponent was my trainer, Nightmaster.

As I made my way to the ring, I recognized a guy from the audience whom I knew from the area's Bally's Total Fitness Club where I had worked as a personal trainer. He stood up and cheered me, but being a "heel," as we call the bad guy in wrestling lingo, I told him to shut up. He quickly sat down with a disappointed look on his face.

During the match itself, Nightmaster used a DDT, a move in which a wrestler holds the opponent in an inverted head-lock, then falls down or backward, slamming the opponent's head into the mat.

Nighmaster won. But at least I had one under my belt.

Even at this basement level of wrestling, politics were a part of the business. T.C. and Frank had a falling-out. It became clear that if I worked for Frank, T.C. wasn't going to train me. Frank, on the other hand, promoted about four or five shows a month. Faced with the decision between training with T.C. in a hayloft or appearing in matches in front of an audience, I chose the latter. My training consisted of working out in the ring before the shows.

I should qualify what I mean by "shows." Usually, we put up the ring in a National Guard armory or other small venue. Crowds varied from two dozen people to a few hundred. One of my favorite venues was the National Guard armory in Hannibal. It was close to home and, because Mark and I helped promote the events, we always drew a strong crowd.

On the business side, sports entertainment is just like any other industry. Success is all about relationships and network-ing. As I worked and gained experience, I also met people who got me booked in other promotions. At that point in my career, building in-ring experience was imperative.

My dilemma was where to train. Performing in matches once a week or so was great, but I needed more formal training. I asked around and learned that Jeff Jarrett was holding classes on Saturday mornings at a gym near Nashville.

Jeff and his dad, Jerry Jarrett, along with the legendary Jerry "the King" Lawler, owned the Memphis-based United States Wrestling Association (USWA), whose productions were a big step up from what I had been doing. So, for the next month or so, I drove the five hours to Nashville every weekend to train with about fifteen others in the class.

While working with Jeff was definitely a step up in my pro wrestling education, I knew that I'd have to devote more than one day a week to training. The problem was that I had no options in my area. However, getting in front of Jeff did help me establish a relationship with USWA management, which led to my first appearance on TV.

One afternoon, after work, I arrived home to a message from Jerry Lawler asking that I call him. Butterflies filled my stomach. I anxiously thought, "This is the break I've been waiting for."

Well, not quite. This "big break" was as generic and bland as it gets. Jerry told me that he wanted me to don a mask and team with another big guy, from southern Missouri, and portray Russian wrestling champions, complete with gold medals.

So, there I was the following Saturday morning in the Channel 5 studios in Memphis proudly representing the USSR, a country that had ceased to exist the year before. The Russian wrestling champions had a squash match on TV against a local tag team that everyone knew didn't stand a chance. A "squash match," in wrestling jargon, means a one-sided match where one side overwhelmingly dominates the other. That Monday, we lost to the team of Reno Riggins and Dutch

Mantel. Today, WWE fans know Mantel as Zeb Colter, who would help me get a number of my early breaks.

The following Saturday, we lost on TV and the team disbanded. Much like our home country, the USSR!

Memphis wrestling had always been known for its outlandish characters and story lines, so I wasn't surprised when I received a call around Christmas from Kevin Lawler, one of Jerry's sons. Kevin had an idea for a seasonal character: the Christmas Creature.

That's right, the Christmas Creature.

Like his father, Kevin was a talented artist; he sent me a rendering. The picture looked like a cross between a Christmas tree and Swamp Thing.

It was all kinds of ridiculous, but it gave me the chance to wrestle against Jerry Lawler, which I knew was a big step in the right direction.

A couple of days later, my mom was back at it, this time making a green full bodysuit, complete with garland, Christmas ornaments, and working Christmas tree lights. The outfit was ahead of its time, with a battery pack to power the miniature light bulbs embedded in the costume.

Needless to say, once the holiday season was over, so was the Christmas Creature!

By now, I was frustrated with my progress—or lack thereof—in the pro-wrestling business. My development was stymied by the lack of places to train and my sporadic work schedule. I was so desperate to get bookings that I traveled once to the Dominican Republic for a weekend—at my own expense—to wrestle a match.

That quick trip was set up by a promoter from Iowa who had connections with Jack Veneno, the biggest name in Dominican Republic wrestling history. I'll never forget seeing pictures on Veneno's office wall of a match between him and Ric Flair in 1982. The photographs featured Veneno holding the National Wrestling Alliance (NWA) World Heavyweight Championship above his head.

Jack Veneno, NWA World Champion? Well, not quite. His "win" was never officially recognized by the NWA. That was because it was never supposed to happen.

Many wrestling fans today know the backstory of this almost mythical match. At its crescendo, it appeared Veneno had defeated Flair and won the championship. However, the time limit had passed, which meant Flair retained the title. When the match finished and Veneno was awarded the title, the crowd went crazy, and Flair knew he'd never get out of there alive if the decision were reversed. He decided that discretion was the better part of valor that particular night and, rather than risk a riot, he let Veneno win.

Of course, there was no internet at the time, and virtually zero media coverage of the event outside the territory. Flair simply returned home with the title as if nothing had happened, and fans were none the wiser. In the Dominican Republic, it was reported that Veneno did not want to leave the country to defend the title, so he gave it back to the NWA.

Although many fans have heard this story, I got to see proof right there on the walls of Jack Veneno's office!

Real Training with the Professor, the Great Malenko

After feeling like I had been spinning my wheels for months, I came to the conclusion that if I was going to be serious about sports entertainment, I would need to make some serious changes.

That would begin with receiving real training.

After doing some research on pro-wrestling schools, I decided to call Malenko's Pro Wrestling Academy in Tampa, Florida, owned and operated by "Professor" Boris Malenko, who had achieved significant success in the 1960s and 1970s. Many fans today are familiar with his talented son, Dean Malenko, whose runs in both WCW and WWE had a big impact.

After talking with the good professor, known in civilian life as Larry Simon, I made up my mind. I was going to Tampa to study wrestling full-time. I borrowed $1,000 from my parents, loaded my belongings into my blue Dodge Diplomat, prayed that the car would make the sixteen-hour trip, and drove off.

When I arrived in Tampa, I met Larry. Everyone who achieves success in anything has help along the way. I've been very fortunate in that respect. Larry helped me as much as anyone. He was one of the kindest and most good-hearted people I have ever met. Larry took me into his home, allowing me to rent a bedroom for a very modest price (I think it was $50 per week); eventually, that rent dropped to zero.

Larry was a source of wisdom and insight. I couldn't have made a better choice. My time with him would prove to be invaluable.

Plus, I was living in beautiful Tampa, just minutes from the beach!

At the school, which was located in a business park, I trained five days a week with other students—from Australia, Britain, and Japan. Larry rented an apartment in the back of the park to his Japanese students. I hit it off with them and spent time driving with them, running errands around town.

Unfortunately, Larry was not in good health. His sons, Dean and Jody, were busy with their own careers. (Today, Dean is still involved with wrestling and Jody is a pharmacist.) They came by occasionally, but most of the day-to-day operations were run by Rico Federico, who worked in WCW and WWE, with Larry providing supervision.

At Malenko's school, we learned more than professional-style wrestling. Larry was long-time friends with Karl Gotch, one of the most legendary grappling and submission practitioners in the history of our business.

To this day, when people think of submission wrestling, they usually think first of Gotch. He had such an influence on pro wrestling in Japan in the 1950s and 1960s that he is still known there as the "God of Wrestling." Because Jody had trained under Gotch, Gotch would sometimes pop into the school.

As a result, there was a strong influence of submission, or "shoot-style," wrestling at Malenko's school. I was finally getting the fundamentals I had lacked—from some of the best our business had ever seen.

Those skills certainly came in handy for the next step in my career.

Japan and a Bear

My first real job in the business was not in traditional professional wrestling, but in shoot-style wrestling, with the Japanese promotion Fujiwara Gumi. It was owned by Yoshiaki Fujiwara, who was considered one of Gotch's best students.

Unlike traditional pro wrestling, which is based around fast-paced action and drama, shoot-style emphasizes pure grappling. In Fujiwara Gumi, you wouldn't see any punches or kicks, or the performers being thrown into the ropes. The action was on the mat with the wrestlers exchanging submission holds along with the occasional judo throw or suplex.

Fujiwara paid me $1,000 a match. That was a godsend at the time. I was working odd jobs to get by during my training, and the money really helped. Fujiwara would fly a few of us from Tampa to Tokyo a few days early, and we'd train at his dojo in preparation for the matches.

Japan was a culture shock for me. One of the things I remember most was that I had to put 100 yen (nearly $1) into a vending machine every hour to watch the hotel TVs! I didn't care to watch it because all the programming was in Japanese.

I was far more interested in training in the dojo and learning from a legend like Yoshiaki Fujiwara.

Fujiwara Gumi held its matches in the world-famous Korakuen Hall, which is part of the legendary Tokyo Dome, the "Tokyo Big Egg." I had a blast at these shows. Unlike audiences elsewhere, the Japanese treat combat arts more like a sporting event to be observed and appreciated. The crowd is often silent, focused on watching the action. To the uninitiated, particularly the wrestlers, this can be unnerving. But once you begin to understand their unique culture with respect to wrestling, you realize the Japanese are just honoring your work.

With my size and strength, and after training with Jody Simon, I could hold my own in the ring against most competition. But what I really enjoyed during that time was watching the other matches.

Fujiwara Gumi was a true mixed martial arts promotion in that they pitted athletes from different disciplines against one another. The contrast in styles was fascinating, especially when the Thai kickboxers fought the wrestlers.

The kickboxers' main offense was to take out the wrestlers' legs with brutal kicks to the outer thighs. Being a grappler myself, I always looked forward to the wrestler weathering the storm, then shooting inside his opponent's defenses and taking him to the ground where the now defenseless kickboxer was quickly forced to submit—unless he could scamper to the ropes to break the hold. It was captivating.

Japan is a school unto itself. Every WWE Superstar I've met who has been lucky enough to visit Japan has told me they appreciated their time there and benefited from it.

Around the holidays, I'd gone back home to visit my folks and friends when I got a phone call from Fujiwara that led to one of the most bizarre things I've ever been involved with in sports entertainment.

Which, when you think about it, is a pretty amazing statement coming from Kane!

Fujiwara was filming a segment for a variety show in Japan. It consisted of footage of him traveling to Canada to train and wrestle...a bear.

You read that right. *A bear!* This wasn't the era of P. T. Barnum and circus sideshow wrestling. It was the 1990s!

Since I was the biggest guy they knew, they asked if I could go to Toronto for a couple of days to be Fujiwara's training partner. In other words, I was going to be the *bear's stunt double*!

I'd had some interesting journeys in my life at that point, even mixing it up once with some future Chicago Bears.

But an actual bear? Different story.

The next thing I knew, I was on a flight to Canada. My part was supposed to be easy—just an hour or so of wrestling with Fujiwara in a training facility. Easy enough, right?

Wrong. Everything went downhill from there.

Evidently, the show's producers forgot that bears hibernate in the winter. That applies to all bears—even the former circus performer who had been trained to "dance" with his human opponents and had been called out of retirement on an exotic animal farm for the scene.

When it came time for them to shoot the fight scene, the bear was having none of it. He hissed and lunged at Fujiwara before dispatching him with a shoulder tackle that sent my mentor flying head over heels.

It was terrible. It was still on YouTube at the time of this writing. I got a chuckle out of watching it again while writing this chapter.

I've seen worse matches, but not many!

Puerto Rico

When I finally got back to Tampa, I received a call from Dutch Mantel. As I mentioned earlier, Dutch was instrumental in helping me early in my career. I'd first met him in Memphis while working for Jerry Lawler and Jerry Jarrett, then ran into him again at an independent show in Illinois, where we exchanged phone numbers. Dutch had just taken over booking for the Puerto Rico territory, and he wanted me to travel to the island to work for him.

I was thrilled. These would not be sporadic, one-off shows. I would finally have the chance to work full-time.

Larry Simon was a lot less excited than I was. There is an old saying in wrestling about promoters. There are two kinds—bad and worse. The Puerto Rico promotion, owned by island legend Carlos Colon, had a reputation as the latter.

That reputation stemmed—rightfully so—from the Bruiser Brody incident just a few years prior. Brody, who had been a top wrestler during the 1980s, was allegedly murdered by another wrestler after a show in 1988, stabbed in the locker room shower. Larry had good reason to be concerned that I would be used and abused in Puerto Rico.

But, despite Larry's concerns, I knew that I had to take the risk. Work was still hard to find, and the opportunity to hone my craft as part of a full-time job was something that I couldn't pass up. Fortunately, it turned out to be a great decision. Carlos was always fair to me, and my time on the island proved rewarding.

That said, I was nervous as I got on the plane in Orlando. Here I was, a Midwestern farm boy headed to a Caribbean island with literally no return ticket and no money; my only contact was a guy I hardly knew. Talk about a roll of the dice!

Things didn't start so well. Dutch had told me someone would meet me at the airport to pick me up. That didn't happen. No one was there. I found a pay phone and called Dutch. He didn't seem surprised and told me to take a cab to his apartment. Luckily, his place wasn't far from the airport, so the cab fare was only a few dollars.

I made my way up to Dutch's apartment, dragging my bags with me, and knocked on the door. An enormous Samoan, his face obscured by his long, wet, curly black hair, opened the door and scowled at me. My greeter was wearing nothing but a lavalava—the traditional skirt worn by many Polynesians—and he filled the entire doorway.

Behind him, a shirtless Dutch Mantel—the man who had talked me into coming to this strange place, the man in whom I had naively placed my trust, the man who had told me that he'd take care of me—was standing on a sofa, shaking his fist and screaming obscenities out of a sliding-glass window.

Welcome to Puerto Rico!

I stood there for a moment in stunned silence, taking in the scene. Just as I was about to write this whole episode off as a case of bad judgment and head back to the airport, preparing to swallow my pride and beg Mom and Dad to buy me a plane ticket home from this nuthouse, I saw a broad grin spread across the Samoan's face.

He extended his hand to shake mine. "Hey, brother, I'm Lloyd," he said warmly. "Sorry, I was just getting out of the shower. Come on in."

As I entered the room, a transformed Dutch jumped off the couch and came over to greet me. He could tell by my expression that I had been caught off guard by the previous scene.

I didn't know then that Lloyd was part of the famous Samoan Anoaʻi family that has produced many WWE Superstars.

I also didn't know Dutch was just acting in character!

He laughed and explained to me that the building next door had been undergoing construction for some time and that the workers had recognized him—asleep on a couch under the picture window—as the dastardly "El Sucio," his television character. Every morning at six, when the workers began, they awakened Dutch with taunts.

Dutch's explanation made all the sense in the world. I immediately felt better. When I asked him later why he didn't just close the window and draw the curtains, he made up some story about having claustrophobia. I didn't buy it. I think he just liked being a heel and enjoyed his interaction with his nemeses across the way.

Puerto Rico was my first real job in the business, and it proved integral to my development as a wrestler. In Japan, I had worn black trunks, pads, and amateur wrestling shoes, and wrestled under my real name. But in Puerto Rico, I wore a hockey mask embossed with a red skull and wrestled as "Doomsday," a homage to the comic book super villain who killed Superman.

Perhaps most important, my creative energies were unleashed in Puerto Rico for the first time. I was allowed to use my imagination and portray a character. I loved it.

To this day, my favorite thing about sports entertainment is its creative aspect. Unlike in other performance arts, in sports entertainment you have the latitude to make a character truly yours. There are few constraints or restrictions. From Ric Flair to Dusty Rhodes to Stone Cold Steve Austin to Undertaker, success is not dependent only on one's ability in the ring and on the mic, but also on one's ability to bring to life a character that the audience can relate to—someone they either love or they love to hate.

There is a beauty and a satisfaction to this known only to my colleagues and few other entertainers.

In Puerto Rico, we worked five days a week, usually Wednesday through Sunday. Unlike Memphis, there were no studio matches. On Wednesday mornings, we taped interviews and promos at the company headquarters. Saturday night was always a big show, and matches from that night were shown on TV the following morning.

I was making a (meager) living doing what I loved, and our apartment was a few feet from the Caribbean Ocean. Life was good!

The fans in Puerto Rico took their wrestling seriously. At times, a little too seriously.

One night at a show, I exited the ring to interact with the fans. An older gentleman pulled out a pocketknife and barreled toward the security barrier. I hightailed it back to the safety of the squared circle.

On another occasion, I witnessed a full-scale riot.

Dutch did a masterful job of booking and storytelling for Carlos's company. Relying on the tried-and-true strategy of uniting his heels into a loose faction or stable, Dutch's business prospered, even as he established himself as the most despised person on the island.

Unfortunately, that position came with legitimate risks.

The hot babyface (good-guy wrestler) at the time was Huracán Castillo Jr., who later competed in WWE as a member of the Hispanic stable Los Boricuas. A long-time heel, Huracán had recently turned babyface, but was not yet accepted in that locker room.

You must understand that in our business, a wrestler without a locker room is like a man without a country. Huracán was taking on Dutch's entire stable alone, which had made him wildly popular with the fans.

It was Saturday night in the Puerto Rican town of Trujillo Alto. The main event was Dutch versus Ray Gonzalez—also a popular young babyface—with Dutch's manager, Joe Don Smith. Smith was locked in a steel cell at ringside.

In attendance was a standing-room-only crowd of more than 3,500. The place was packed and electric. As we pulled into the parking lot, which was already full a couple of hours before the show, Dutch whispered softly to himself, "I've got a bad feeling about this."

I guess it was a premonition.

The story line to that point was that Dutch had severely beaten and injured Castillo, which explained why Huracán wasn't at the show. The main event rolled around and Dutch took a beating from Ray before Joe Don was able to slip Dutch some brass knuckles between the bars of his cage. Dutch hit Ray with the brass knuckles to win the match. Dutch then unlocked Joe Don's cage and the two of them put the boots to Ray.

That's when Huracán Castillo made a surprise entrance and came to Ray's rescue. The roof blew off the place.

Castillo blew through Joe Don Smith and snatched Dutch. The crowd had been hoping for this moment all night! The place went bonkers when Castillo started to pummel Dutch. Every time he punched Dutch, the audience cheered.

Fans began converging on the ring, blocking the aisles and escape routes. Just then, Lloyd and another stablemate, Louie Fabiano, hit the ring. Castillo fought them off, but Dutch was able to use the distraction to escape to our locker room.

As he made his way back toward the ring, Dutch tripped over some of the fans who were blocking his path. He went face-first into the edge of the bleachers, badly cutting himself around the eye. I was watching the entire scene from just outside the locker room and grabbed Dutch to help him back. After getting Dutch back into the locker room, I opened the door to go back out.

It was pure chaos. The building was now filled with an angry, unruly mob.

Joe Don, Lloyd, and Louie were trapped in the ring which, at this point, was probably the safest place in the building. The hall outside our locker room was filled with fans who were pushing and shoving the security guards. One of the security guards had his jacket pulled up from the bottom over his head and shoulders much like you see in a hockey fight. He was fighting a losing battle with fans trying to disrobe him.

I pulled him into the safety of the locker room. Even though he was holding a towel against his bloody eye, Dutch laughed when my only comment about the entire scene engulfing the both of us was "Wow."

Luckily, the police showed up shortly thereafter, and things de-escalated quickly. We took Dutch to the hospital, where he got a couple dozen stitches to sew up the cuts above and below his eye.

That event was intense. All in all, that was probably the most exciting night of my career, but not in a good way, nor one that I would ever want to experience again.

Still, my overall experience in Puerto Rico was great. I ended up working there for about nine months. I was gaining experience in the ring while living in the Caribbean. Not a bad deal at all!

At one point, "Hot Stuff" Eddie Gilbert moved into our apartment. Eddie had worked in promotions around the world as both an in-ring performer and a booker. He was widely acknowledged as one of the great minds in the wrestling business, and I had the good fortune to be around him for a few months.

It was in Puerto Rico that I also had my first match with Mick Foley, whose ring name was Cactus Jack, when he traveled to the island for a couple of shows. I can't say enough about him, both as a performer and a person.

Life is filled with inflection points, events that may seem insignificant at the time but change the course of your entire career. One of those moments for me had occurred when I was standing in the doorway of Lloyd Anoaʻi's apartment watching Dutch scream out the window and wondering what I was doing there.

Thank goodness that Lloyd extended his hand and invited me into his home. Otherwise, my life would have never been the same.

Smoky Mountain Wrestling

After runs with every babyface on the roster in Puerto Rico, I felt that it was time to take the next step in my nascent career. Dutch agreed and called his old friend, Jim Cornette, owner of the Knoxville, Tennessee–based Smoky Mountain Wrestling (SMW).

Many fans know that, along with the late Bobby "the Brain" Heenan, Cornette is considered one of the greatest managers and minds in the history of professional wrestling. His work with the legendary tag team The Midnight Express in

Mid-South Wrestling and Jim Crockett Promotions in the 1980s is still talked about today.

Needless to say, I was excited by the idea of working for him. Cornette was intrigued by the thought of a big guy like me working for SMW.

Since he was also working with WWE as a creative consultant and managing the tag team The Heavenly Bodies, Cornette realized that I was exactly the kind of talent WWE was looking for and that he could help me through his promotion.

Cornette told me that I would start right after Christmas. In the meantime, Eddie Gilbert had arranged for me to work for Otto Wanz in Germany.

Wanz was a significant name in wrestling in Germany and was also famous for having the Guinness World Record for tearing up telephone books! Arnold Schwarzenegger cites Wanz, who was always performing feats of strength, as one of his early influences.

Wanz's touring model was different from any others I'd come across. For instance, USWA had a set weekly touring schedule. You'd be in Memphis for TV on Saturday morning then Nashville that night. Sunday was a small show somewhere, then Monday was Memphis at the Mid-South Coliseum. Tuesday was at the Louisville Gardens, and Wednesday at the Evansville Memorial Coliseum. Smoky Mountain Wrestling taped a month of TV programming at one time in different venues every month and had no set weekly routine. WWE, of course, is constantly on the road at different arenas all the time.

Wanz didn't have a TV show. All of his promotion was

local. The shows were held at the same venue for about a month, and then the operation moved to the next city for a month.

There were other differences as well. Much like in boxing, the matches were segmented into rounds and you could win by knockout. Otto's ring was also as hard as concrete and just as unforgiving, so you didn't see many high-impact moves.

I spent the coldest November of my life in Bremen, Germany. Literally. Most of the wrestlers lived out back of the arena in campers. Mine didn't have heat or a bathroom. I showered and used the toilet in the arena. I'd huddle under the covers at night and hope that I didn't have to use the bathroom before the arena opened in the morning.

Nonetheless, working for Otto was a blast. I met folks like the English pro wrestler Tony St. Clair and Dave "Fit" Finlay, the wrestler and trainer from Northern Ireland.

I also formed a tag team with John Layfield, aka Justin "Hawk" Bradshaw, later known as JBL in WWE. We were called the "Zwei Metre" tag team, which loosely translated to "the six-foot-six team." We dominated the competition and formed a friendship during our time there that continues to this day.

After my run in Germany, I flew back to the United States to spend the holidays with my family before traveling to Knoxville to work with Smoky Mountain Wrestling. I was anxious to begin.

Smoky Mountain was truly an all-star promotion, boasting a great talent pool with performers like Ricky Morton and Robert Gibson of the WWE Hall of Fame tag team, The

Rock 'n' Roll Express; Tracy Smothers; Tony Anthony; the famous wrestling family the Armstrongs (which included future WWE star "Road Dogg" Jesse James), The Heavenly Bodies, Chris Candido along with his manager Tammy Sytch (later known as Sunny in WWE), and others. Arn Anderson had just finished a run with SMW. So had Cactus Jack, Chris Jericho, and Lance Storm.

Cornette informed me that I would be forming a tag team with Eddie Gilbert, one of my mentors from Puerto Rico. Cornette dubbed me Unabomb, which was not a reference to Ted Kaczynski, the domestic terrorist who had sent explosive packages to innocent people in the mail and became known as the Unabomber. Cornette chose the name simply because he thought it sounded cool.

Just as I had done in Puerto Rico, I wore a hockey mask into the ring, but took it off for the match.

Best of all, Eddie and I were immediately thrown into a story line with Ricky and Robert! I was getting a rivalry with The Rock 'n' Roll Express! Talk about pumped.

In early 1995, when I arrived in Knoxville to work for Cornette, I had no idea how much my life would change. I figured I would return home to the St. Louis area when my Smoky Mountain run was over, but that didn't happen.

Instead, East Tennessee was where I met my wife, raised a family, and built my life.

My first night in Knoxville, I split a room with Eddie at a hotel on Asheville Highway. The next day, we drove to SMW's monthly TV taping outside Knoxville. The day included matches and promos, all of which were edited together for TV stations across the Southeast. After a long day of matches and promos, Eddie headed back to his home in West Tennessee while I stayed with some of the guys in an apartment they had rented.

Within a week, Eddie called to tell me that he was taking over as the booker for Carlos Colon in Puerto Rico and was leaving immediately. This presented me with a real problem. We had just taped a month of TV featuring the two of us as a tag team and setting up an angle (wrestling jargon for a story line) with Ricky and Robert. In fact, our first live match was against them that weekend in Knoxville.

Tragically, Eddie died from a heart attack shortly after returning to Puerto Rico. He was thirty-three years old.

Cornette ended up switching the tag team match to a singles contest between Ricky and me. There were a couple of thousand people in the Knoxville Civic Coliseum, but to me, it might as well have been a sellout at Madison Square Garden. The arena looked huge and packed.

Puerto Rico and Germany had been great, but this was different. I was in the ring with Ricky Morton, a guy whom I had watched on TV, and I was in front of a good crowd in a real arena. It was a far cry from working in front of a few dozen people in a high school gym or National Guard armory.

For the first time, I felt like a star. I really felt like a professional wrestler.

Today, the office I occupy as mayor is across the street from the Knoxville Civic Coliseum. I see it every time I arrive and every time I leave. Literally every day, I drive to work, and it feels like I'm heading back there for my first match with Ricky Morton.

Who would have thought, when that match was going down in 1995, that a little more than twenty years later I would be mayor of this place!

That night, I lost my match to Ricky because of a disqualification. While my performance wasn't stellar, especially compared with someone as talented and experienced as Ricky Morton, it was nevertheless more than adequate. During the next couple of weeks, I was booked against Ricky in smaller towns, back in the high school gyms and National Guard armories.

Meanwhile, Cornette was busy finding me a new partner, and I got busy trying to find myself a more permanent housing arrangement.

Crystal

We jokingly referred to the apartment where I had spent a couple of nights on the sofa as the Smoky Mountain Wrestling flophouse. Wrestler Anthony LoMonaco had his name on the lease, but he was a sport about helping other guys out by letting them stay there. Unfortunately for me, all the bedrooms were taken, so I set out to find my own apartment.

The first place I moved to was a one-room efficiency apartment out in the country. It was cheap, but also pretty depressing. I was there by myself, and my only social interactions occurred during my daily time at the gym. After about a month, I found another apartment in town and split the rent with SMW's Boo Bradley, who would go on to become Balls Mahoney for Extreme Championship Wrestling (ECW).

Though I was not living there, I found almost a second home in Anthony's apartment—aka the SMW flophouse!—which served as a gathering place for transplants like me from other areas of the country.

Then one evening, a friend of Anthony's stopped by.

Crystal Parker was accompanied by her two daughters, Devan and Arista, eleven and eight, respectively. Anthony occasionally babysat for the kids while Crystal was at work or school. I was immediately smitten by this beautiful woman whose red hair flowed out from under her Minnie Mouse ball cap.

A couple of months later, wrestler D'Lo Brown suggested that I ask her out. I did.

Not only was Crystal beautiful, she was smart, hardworking, determined, and kindhearted. When I met her, Crystal was working on her master's degree in counseling from East Tennessee State University. At the same time, she was working full-time as a social worker, part-time at a convenience store in the evenings, and waiting tables at her mom's restaurant outside of Knoxville on the weekends. All this while raising two daughters.

On our first date, we went to eat at the Bennigan's in Johnson City, Tennessee, where Crystal was living. Not very romantic, I know, but it was all that I could afford. Crystal and I hit it off very well.

We spent as much time together as our busy schedules

would allow. Devan, her older daughter, had broken her leg in a bicycle accident and spent weeks in the hospital with her leg in traction, so much of our early courtship involved passing time with Devan in the hospital, watching scary movies and playing board games.

After a couple of months, Crystal and I decided to get married. That was in August 1995. Moving into the cramped little house where Crystal was living with her two daughters was a culture shock for me. Devan and Arista have very different personalities, and they often fought like cats and dogs. Our house was loud and chaotic at times. It was also fun and spontaneous. You never knew what Devan, the wild child, would be up to.

Like all couples, Crysal and I have had our ups and downs. As my career progressed, I spent much more time on the road than I did at home. That will cause strain within any marriage. But Crystal has always been a rock, strong and steady. She ran the household, usually while working full-time. To this day, she is the hardest-working person I have ever met. She is also the most caring person I know. Like me, she's a big dog lover. Over the years, we have adopted dozens of fur babies—in a couple of cases, animals which had been severly neglected or abused.

Just like their mom, my daughters are talented, hardworking young women. Both of them are nurses with postgraduate degrees. Devan is a nurse practitioner who works for a cardiac recovery group. Arista manages operations for a home health service in a neighboring county.

Oh, and did I mention that I'm a grandpa? Yep, two

grandchildren. And, yes, it's true—grandkids are the best gift in the entire world!

Al Snow

By the time the next set of monthly TV tapings rolled around in Lenoir, North Carolina, Cornette had found a new tag team partner for me: Al Snow.

Al was a hot commodity on the independent circuit. He was talented and versatile in the ring and great on the mic, with a cocky in-ring persona. Behind the scenes, he was an intelligent, down-to-earth guy with an easygoing personality and a great sense of humor. Teaming with Al was an education for me, his years of experience compensating for my lack of it.

Cornette called us The Dynamic Duo, but we got off to a bit of a rocky start.

Al had just driven in from his home in Lima, Ohio, an eight-hour trip. In his first match on TV, he faced the veteran wrestler George South. George had never been a big name, but he was a terrific performer who had wrestled all around the world, including for WCW and WWE. Ric Flair even once said George was "my favorite guy to work on TV."

If you ever watched the *World Championship Wrestling* NWA TV show that came on at 6:05 p.m. ET on Superstation WTBS every Saturday, whether you watched it back in the 1980s or on the WWE Network today, you have seen George South wrestle.

Cornette wanted their match to be filled with action that showcased Al's in-ring abilities. That wasn't the match he got.

Al, exhausted from his drive, was doing his best to establish his heel persona. We all watched on the monitor backstage as Al ran from George, jumped out of the ring to get away from him, and tried, in a faux show of sportsmanship, to persuade George to shake his hand.

Because pro wrestling is an art form and very subjective, wrestlers sometimes differ on a vision for the match. What do you want out of this? How do you go about portraying that to the audience? These are important, creative questions for which there are usually different answers.

A guy like Jim Cornette is acutely aware of these dynamics, so he patiently explained to Al and George that what he had seen in their first match wasn't what he was looking for. He wanted lots of action to show Al's athletic and wrestling prowess. He directed them to go back out and put on a short match with a series of high spots (wrestling parlance for good action), and he would edit the two matches together for television.

When they went back out, the match only lasted about a minute, not the five minutes Cornette had asked for.

At this time, I was unaware that Cornette possessed an explosive temper that was legendary in the wrestling business. When Al and George finished their match, Cornette stared at the monitor for a full thirty seconds, repeating, "Is that it?" over and over.

That was when Cornette went from hot to nuclear.

His face began to change color. First red, then dark scarlet, before ultimately turning bright purple. As Cornette's rage escalated, the other wrestlers ducked out of the room. I had never seen a conniption fit before and it was something to behold. Cornette sputtered and frothed, kicking at the furniture in the room, and spitting out curses.

Then, the most amazing thing happened. Al and George walked into the room and Cornette reverted instantly to normal behavior. The man who had been a raging beast just a few seconds earlier told them in a voice as calm as a gentle summer breeze, "Guys, that wasn't really what I wanted, but I'll make it work."

Fortunately, the rest of the night went like clockwork. And, thanks to the magic of TV, Al's match with George looked seamless and got the point across. Al Snow was the real deal, and The Dynamic Duo was off to a great start.

Meeting Vince

When I arrived at SMW, "Good Ol' J.R." Jim Ross, a future Hall of Fame announcer, was on hiatus from WWE and working as Cornette's TV announcer. J.R. took an immediate liking to me and, within a couple of months, had arranged a tryout match with WWE. To the best of my recollection, I believe it took place in Macon, Georgia.

There, I talked briefly with Vince McMahon, whom you know as WWE's Chairman and CEO. I had always been taught that wrestlers were supposed to shake hands lightly with one another. When I went to shake hands with Vince in this traditional way, he immediately corrected me, warmly advising me to shake hands firmly with everyone I met.

49

There was nothing mean or menacing about his remark; it was simply a bit of advice, and one that I've never forgotten.

My match that night was against Reno Riggins, whom I had met a couple of years before. As in dancing, good matches require two competent performers to work well together. Luckily I had a good, experienced partner in Reno. That day, he helped me deliver a great showing, one that included leap-frogs, dropkicks, and other athletic maneuvers.

At the next SMW show, Cornette told me that WWE had been extremely impressed with my performance and that I should expect a phone call from them shortly.

I was ecstatic!

When I wasn't on the road wrestling, I was spending more and more time with Crystal. That wasn't always an easy task. She was working multiple jobs on top of her schoolwork, and Devan required special attention after the bicycle accident.

But, overall, things were going along well. Al and I were competing for, and eventually won, the SMW tag team championship. I had fallen in love with a wonderful woman and her family. I was happy.

Then the phone call from WWE—the one that Cornette had told me to expect—finally came.

Vince Gives the Good News—and the Bad

That was on April 19, 1995. I remember the date well because I can recall turning on the TV that day to see Oklahoma

City's Alfred P. Murrah Federal Building in ruins, demolished by an act of terror that killed 168 people and shocked the nation.

WWE's J.J. Dillon informed me that Vince McMahon wanted to meet with me. A few weeks later, I flew from Knoxville to LaGuardia Airport in New York. There, a limousine took me to the WWE offices in nearby Stamford, Connecticut.

Now, before that, I had never been in a limousine. "I'm going to be a WWE Superstar," I thought to myself. Just like Ric Flair, I'd be limousine riding and jet flying!

I arrived at WWE headquarters and was taken up to J.J.'s office. Vince walked in a couple of minutes later. After some small talk, we settled down to business.

Vince wanted me to work for WWE, but he also wanted me to become more polished and to gain more experience, so he offered me a developmental contract. I would continue to work for SMW with WWE subsidizing my pay there with a modest stipend. That sounded reasonable to me and I verbally accepted.

I felt like I was on a rocket ship. I'd just been chauffeured in a limo. Now I had a contract with WWE—not a big-money deal, but a contract nevertheless!

Then my rocket ship blew an engine and plummeted earthward.

Vince informed me that he had a character idea in mind that he'd wanted to do for a while.

Next, he asked me, "Are you afraid of the dentist?"

Now, I'd heard lots of stories from other wrestlers about how Vince was a master of getting inside your head, kind of an evil genius who could tell you what you were thinking before you thought it, but I had no idea what the point of his question was, so I simply answered, "No, sir."

He chuckled and told me his idea: a wrestling dentist named Isaac Yankem. "I yank 'em," Vince laughed in his Vince laugh. "You'll be perfect for it," he told me as he got up to leave.

One of the things that Eddie Gilbert taught me was to maintain a poker face when presented with match finishes, story lines, and pretty much everything else in wrestling. You put yourself at a disadvantage if you let anyone know that you are unhappy with a situation. Many wrestlers earn a bad reputation by "putting on the boo-boo face" when they are unhappy with their role, instead of adopting a professional demeanor.

I kept Eddie's lesson in mind as I sat there digesting what Vince had just told me. On the outside, I did my best to act excited for this opportunity. On the inside, my emotions were completely different.

From the start, I hated the idea of Isaac Yankem. Here I was, six foot eight and 315 pounds, and Vince McMahon wanted me to be a ridiculous, wrestling dentist. "This is a nightmare," I thought. I chastised myself, sure that I had just made an enormous mistake.

How in the world was I ever going to get over being a wrestling dentist? In my mind, that character was destined for failure before it happened.

Looking back, of course, my attitude wasn't very constructive. In fact, I was being a prima donna. With the luxury of hindsight, I now realize how fortunate I was. Most wrestlers never get to see the inside of WWE headquarters, much less sit down and talk with Vince McMahon, much less sign with the company.

I didn't think about it at the time, but I still had a lot to learn. I was also still a long way from being the performer I would one day become.

Isaac Yankem gave me the ability to fail while I was learning. While I still don't much like the character, I understand today that it was a step I had to take. My later success would never have occurred had I not played that role in WWE first.

Back in SMW, The Dynamic Duo was hot. Al and I continued our rivalry with The Rock 'n' Roll Express and also had a nice program with Tracy Smothers and Tony Anthony. We also worked against the Armstrong family—"Bullet" Bob and his son, Brian aka "Road Dogg" Jesse James.

Although I never wrestled him, I also loved to watch Brad Armstrong, another of Bob's sons. Along with Ricky Steamboat, Brad was the best pure babyface I've ever seen.

WWE sometimes loaned its stars to SMW. In fact, the night that Al and I won the SMW tag team championship, Undertaker was on the card. That show was *Bluegrass Brawl III* on April 7, 1995, in Pikeville, Kentucky. Al and I defeated Ricky and Robert that night in a Coal Miner's Glove Match.

It was my first championship in sports entertainment.

But the real draw that night was The Gangstas and D'Lo Brown versus Tracy Smothers and Undertaker in a 3-on-2

Handicap Match. The buildup to that match was phenomenal, with Cornette displaying his incomparable creative talent, including producing one of the most memorable vignettes I have ever seen.

It featured Undertaker digging a grave while Blue Öyster Cult's "(Don't Fear) the Reaper" played in the background. In his deep, macabre voice, Undertaker sent a message to The Gangstas, who draped gang flags over the bodies of their fallen victims following their matches.

As he shoveled, Undertaker said, "Gangstas, you bury your victims under a flag. I bury mine under six feet of cold hard dirt." Genius!

While SMW appeared in markets like Knoxville and Johnson City, we spent most of our time in small towns throughout Appalachia. Some of them were so small that I referred to them as "Witness Protection Towns." If you were in the FBI's witness protection program, you'd be safe there because most people don't know these places even exist!

Towns like Princeton, West Virginia; Council, Virginia; and West Liberty, Kentucky. Every town had a story and you never knew what you'd learn.

For instance, one evening we pulled into Flatwoods, Kentucky, population 7,000. As we drove into town, we were welcomed by this sign: WELCOME TO FLATWOODS, it read in big letters. HOME OF BILLY RAY CYRUS. Unfortunately, Billy Ray didn't make it to the show that night. Neither did most of the rest of Flatwoods, as our crowd numbered only a few dozen.

The highlight of my SMW career came on August 4, 1995,

at the Knoxville Civic Coliseum, in front of five thousand people.

That night was the first of what would be many matches against Undertaker.

The *Superbowl of Wrestling* was an all-star show featuring not only Undertaker, but also Shawn Michaels. I had met Undertaker—Mark Calaway—a couple of times before, but this was the first time that I had a chance to spend time with him. Even as heralded as he is, Mark's understanding of pro-wrestling psychology is probably not as appreciated as it should be.

The Undertaker character is so strong that half the battle is getting the crowd to accept that Undertaker is in jeopardy at any point in the match—especially when he's wrestling an unknown commodity like me!

Taker structured the match that night in such a way that the crowd bought into me taking the fight to him. It worked. Despite my nerves—after all, this was the biggest match of my career, by far—we pulled off a good showing. Of course, most of it was due to the popularity of Undertaker, but I did my part.

For me, the most important outcome of that night was proving to Mark that I had the talent to be in the ring with him. For the rest of my career, Mark Calaway would be one of my biggest advocates, and for that I am forever grateful to him. Trust me, having Undertaker in your corner is some powerful mojo.

A week later, I had my last match in SMW at *Fire on the Mountain* in Johnson City, where I lost a Loser Leaves Town Match.

That night was bittersweet. I was headed to WWE, which had been my goal since entering sports entertainment. But I was comfortable at SMW, had made some good friends there, and would miss them.

Since SMW was a regional promotion, I could drive to nearly every town from home and back again in a short period of time, so I was usually at home every night, which allowed me to spend time with Crystal and the kids. That would change in WWE, where you sometimes spend weeks at a time on the road.

Nevertheless, whether I was ready for it or not, the next chapter in my life was about to begin.

CHAPTER 3

ISAAC YANKEM, DDS

Fireworks rocked the Pittsburgh Civic Arena—aka "the Igloo"—as Bret "Hit Man" Hart made his grand entrance into the ring at WWE's *SummerSlam* in August 1995. On the other side of the ring stood his opponent.

Me!

Earlier that month, while still wrestling in SMW, I had traveled to Stamford to meet with representatives of WWE's Creative Services. They showed me the outfit they had designed for my new alter ego, Isaac Yankem, DDS. The costume consisted of black boots, blue pants, and a white lab smock that served as a ring jacket. They also provided me with a headpiece equipped with a magnifying lens like the one used by a dentist and a black leather medical bag.

Finally, they told me that Vince thought it would be ironic if his wrestling dentist had poor oral hygiene, so they gave me a couple of bottles of black and brown acrylic paint. We experimented with painting my teeth to give them a decayed look.

While I was there, I met Howard Finkel, WWE's long-time ring announcer. Howard informed me that he had suggested Needles, Washington, as Isaac Yankem's hometown, but Vince liked Decatur, Illinois.

Get it? "Decay-tour"?

Just when I thought it couldn't get any worse, I heard my entrance music for the first time. Instead of a cool rock song with powerful guitar riffs and pounding drums, my "music" was the sound of a dentist's drill whirling away!

After meeting with Creative Services, I filmed a series of vignettes in Stamford at a real dentist's office. Isaac Yankem was made out to be Jerry Lawler's personal dentist. After losing a "kiss my foot" match with Bret Hart, Lawler was using Yankem's wrestling services to exact revenge on the Hit Man.

The vignettes portrayed me, along with Lawler, pulling my patients' teeth, sans anesthesia, of course. The last one was pretty cute. It was simply an answering machine with the message that my office was closed until I dispatched Bret Hart at *SummerSlam*.

The Friday before the match, I met Bill Watts and Bret at WWE's training facility to put together the *SummerSlam* match. Watts had recently joined WWE to replace J.J. Dillon as head of Talent Relations. J.J. had recently departed to work for WCW—an early shot across the bow in the Monday Night War.

Watts, the promoter and wrestler of Mid-South Wrestling, was famous for his no-nonsense demeanor. After working out that day, I felt that we had a good game plan for *SummerSlam*. The next day, I flew to Pittsburgh, picked up a rental car, and checked into a Red Roof Inn, where I was reunited with my friend from Puerto Rico and now my travel partner, Dutch Mantel.

The *SummerSlam* match was passable. Of course, it didn't hurt that I was in the ring with Bret Hart, one of the greatest performers ever. Still, I did my part, too.

Unfortunately, I was unhappy with the Yankem character and having trouble adjusting to WWE, the big league of sports entertainment. After all, a few short months before, I had been watching people like Bret Hart on TV. Now I was a peer. It was a difficult transition for me, and the *SummerSlam* match against Bret proved to be the highlight of Yankem's WWE run.

The night after *SummerSlam* was a live *Monday Night Raw* in Erie, Pennsylvania. I had an enhancement match (a short, one-sided match meant to build the winner's allure) during which I beat a young Scott Taylor, the future Scotty 2 Hotty of Too Cool fame. Our match was terrible and everyone, including me, knew it. The cracks were showing.

After debuting as a featured performer with Bret at *SummerSlam*, I was soon relegated to midcard status. My WWE career seemed to be spiraling downward before it had even started. Occasionally, I showed flashes of brilliance, but for the most part, my matches were uninspired mediocrity.

After one particularly bad performance during a TV match against him, Undertaker pulled me aside for a come-to-Jesus talk. "Look," he told me point-blank, "you have to start acting like you belong here. Vince likes you, but you *have* to get more aggressive or you won't make it."

Not long after that, Vince himself would give me a similar talk.

An Important Lesson

I had a decision to make. I could continue to mope around feeling sorry for myself because I was saddled with a character that I hated, or I could make the most of what I had and do the best that I could to prove I belonged in WWE.

I chose the latter, and that decision saved my career.

My matches got better, and WWE kept me busy on TV and live events, usually in the role of "jobber to the stars." In other words, my role was to provide top talent with a competitive opponent.

The term "jobber" is not one I use a lot. The connotation is degrading and disrespectful. Not everyone is going to be a star in the wrestling business, but I think that everyone in the wrestling business deserves at least a modicum of respect from their colleagues and fans for their willingness to get out there and try.

I've seen "job guys" who are tremendously talented but have just never gotten their break. I've also seen "stars" whose work was mediocre and who treated their colleagues and fans like dirt.

Besides, without jobbers—people who make the stars look good—where would the business be?

Around this time, WWE was experiencing the rise of a group soon to be known as The Kliq: Shawn Michaels, Triple

H (still "Hunter Hearst Helmsley" back then), Scott Hall, Kevin Nash, and Sean Waltman.

In fact, The Kliq wasn't the only clique in the locker room. Several groups of guys traveled and hung out together. Nor, in my opinion, was The Kliq as divisive as they are sometimes portrayed. Did they wield a lot of power? Yes, but so did a guy like Undertaker, and he and The Kliq always got along fine.

I never had a problem with them. In fact, Shawn and Kevin went out of their way to make me look good in my matches with them. Triple H and I were occasional travel partners. Sean Waltman would later become one of my favorite tag team partners.

Did The Kliq target people they didn't like? Probably. But here's the reality about WWE and, for that matter, everything else that involves human beings: Politics are part of it, and if you want to be successful, you'd better be able to navigate your way through. This is true in everything, from the business world to professional sports. From what I saw of The Kliq, if they thought you could draw money and you tried to get along with them, things were fine. At least they were in my case.

WWE is truly a global company. During my stint as Isaac Yankem, DDS, I performed in Europe, India, Kuwait, and South Africa. With WWE's intense touring schedule, we were rarely anywhere for more than a day, so it was a nice change to spend a couple days at the Sun City resort in South Africa in preparation for a pay-per-view special.

Sun City boasted a massive water park and world-class

golf. I'm not much of a golfer, but I couldn't resist hitting the links when I heard crocodiles inhabited the water hazards!

It was set up in such a way that the crocs couldn't get to the players, or anyone else, but I had to see them!

Fake Diesel

While we were in South Africa, Jerry Brisco, then a WWE road agent, told me to call Vince when I returned stateside. Road agents are WWE staffers, often former wrestlers, who produce matches, look after talent during shows, and serve as a conduit between the office and the talent. I called the office as soon as I arrived home.

Ann Russo with Talent Relations informed me that Vince had an idea for me. WCW, our main competitor, had recently lured away two of WWE's biggest stars, Scott Hall and Kevin Nash. In WWE, Hall was Razor Ramon and Nash was Diesel. Vince wanted WWE commentator Jim Ross (aka J.R.) to portray a bitter, vengeful employee determined to prove that he was the one responsible for WWE's success. In the story line, J.R. recruited a new Razor, portrayed by Rick Bognar. Vince wanted me to become what everyone would call "fake" Diesel.

The story line was that J.R. had presented a "new" Ramon and Diesel to the fans to show he was the real star maker in the company. J.R. would prove to the world that he, not Vince, was the creative genius behind WWE.

I was excited about the story line, which I saw as an opportunity to shed the Isaac Yankem character and move on to something different. I had matured both in the ring and outside of it. By this time, I was confident that I belonged in WWE, but I believed that the Yankem character carried too much baggage to allow me to shine.

In life, having confidence in one's abilities is often what makes you or breaks you. I've found that to be true in sports and business. If you convince yourself that you're capable of doing something, you stand a good chance of achieving your goal, even if you don't actually possess all the necessary skills or tools. Likewise, you can have everything you need to succeed, but if you don't believe in yourself, you can sabotage your own success.

The same was true when I decided to run for mayor. I really had no idea what I was doing. It was completely different from anything I had ever done. People would suggest things throughout the campaign and I would be like, "That sounds like a good idea. I think I'll try it!"

Because I had confidence, I wasn't afraid to take risks. We ran our entire campaign by the seats of our pants. I wasn't a seasoned politician, and that was a big part of my appeal.

I believed in myself and was always willing to do unconventional things. Though my lack of political experience scared me at times, I filled those voids with life lessons I had learned in WWE.

Not to mention, I used my sports entertainment persona to strengthen my political appeal. I brought WWE Superstars like Ric Flair, Undertaker, Big Show, Daniel Bryan, Matt Hardy, Mark Henry—and Ricky Morton!—and others into Knoxville for campaign-related appearances.

I was determined to be a different kind of candidate because I was confident. Various veteran political "experts" would advise that I shouldn't do this or that. Whatever they told me not to do, that was usually exactly what I did!

If I had listened to any of the people who wanted to treat me like a vanilla candidate, I would have had a hard time succeeding. I went with my gut, because I knew how to connect with people better than they did.

I knew what would work.

I knew this, in part, because I didn't know what I was doing! Now, I'm not saying I didn't accept good advice or listen to others. I would have been a fool not to.

But I always remembered what an old high school coach told me. Because I wasn't an aggressive person, he told me I needed to step outside of my personality. He said I needed to get out of my comfort zone.

In running for office, I did just that—in a big way. But I was always confident and it worked!

Similarly, over twenty years ago I made a conscious decision that I was going to be a WWE Superstar, no matter what. That doesn't mean that I knew everything or could handle any situation flawlessly. It just meant that I followed the old adage, "Fake it until you make it."

By the time the new Razor and Diesel debuted, my in-ring work had noticeably improved. Backstage, I was treated differently, not necessarily like a top star, but much more deferentially than when I was the dentist.

Even Vince made a point to applaud my performance and new attitude.

Unfortunately, WWE fans rejected the entire story line. Conceptually, it wasn't a bad idea, but instead of embracing the underlying plot line, which was somewhat complex and confusing, they refused to accept the new Razor and Diesel as anything but imitations of the originals.

It didn't help that J.R. was a popular character who was hard to dislike.

People ask me what Kevin Nash thought about the gimmick. I don't think that he and I have ever really discussed it. Besides, the story line was not intended to ridicule Kevin and Scott in any way. WWE treated Rick and me as serious competitors, even championship contenders, not as bumbling buffoons there to poke fun at. It was just one of those things that happens so often in the world of sports entertainment: an off-the-wall idea that never found legs.

Around this time, WWE established a working relationship with Mexico's AAA promotion. A number of AAA stars appeared on WWE programming, most notably their Mini-Estrella luchador versions of WWE Superstars like Vader, Mankind, and Goldust. In exchange, WWE sent Rick and me to work in Mexico on and off for a few months.

In Mexico, we wrestled a lot in traditional Six-Man Two-Out-of-Three Falls matches with Lucha Libre legends like Perro Aguayo and Pierroth Jr. While it wasn't exactly WWE, I enjoyed learning the Lucha Libre style and tradition.

One particular trip to Mexico proved very eventful.

I flew from home to Mexico City, where we had a match that night. The next day, everyone flew to Juarez to work that evening. When we arrived in Juarez, we had to go through an immigration checkpoint, which was strange since it was a domestic flight. The Mexican immigration officials gave Rick and me a difficult time before allowing us to go on. We performed at the show in Juarez that night, but the next day, things took an unexpected turn.

The following morning, we returned to Juarez to catch a flight back to Mexico City. The same immigration officials who had been there the day before were checking passports. Again, this was strange, since passports are not usually required to board domestic flights.

In any case, Rick and I were told there was a problem with our passports and we were not allowed to board the plane. The officers told us to return to the airport in a couple of hours to meet with their supervisor and straighten things out.

We returned to our hotel, which was a short walk from the American border.

In search of a pay phone, I crossed the bridge over the Rio Grande River leading into El Paso. Remember, this is 1997, long before cell phones were ubiquitous. First, I tried calling the AAA office, but no one picked up. I then called WWE and explained the situation. They put me on with their in-house immigration attorney. He instructed me to cooperate with the Mexican officials and said we'd get everything worked out.

When Rick and I returned to the airport, the immigration officials loaded us into a beat-up Crown Victoria and drove us to their headquarters. The HQ was located at the base of the bridge to the United States, the same bridge I'd crossed earlier that day.

In the office, the supervisor asked for our passports and

looked them over. He then informed us that we were working in Mexico illegally. The papers in our passports were not
work visas. They were *applications* for work visas. The visas
had never been issued. There was obviously a mix-up, I said;
we could get everything straightened out when we got back to
the United States.

He replied with the most terrifying words I have ever
heard: "Oh, you can't leave."

My mind immediately began racing. Simply put, going to
jail in Mexico wasn't high on my bucket list, to say the least.
Within a second, I had devised a plan, basically taking out the
officers at the knees and sprinting across the bridge, leaping
into the arms of the first American border guard I could find.

Luckily, nothing that dramatic occurred. We were fined a
modest sum, which required a wire transfer from WWE, since
the Mexican officials couldn't process credit cards, then given
back our passports and sent on our way.

While I laugh about it now, I'll never forget the sink-
ing feeling of seeing my passport in that official's hands and
knowing I was completely at his mercy.

Rick and I finished our run in Mexico, and then began
working for USWA and my former dental patient, Jerry
Lawler!

Then I got a call that would change my life.

CHAPTER 4

THE BIG RED MACHINE IN THE ATTITUDE ERA

There are arguably few better "right time, right place" scenarios in the history of sports entertainment. Vince already liked my work and me personally and was looking for a worthy opponent for Undertaker.

I was past ready to finally make my mark. I'll never forget how it all came together. Or, I guess I should say, I'll never forget how nearly all of it came together.

Creating Kane

While still on loan from WWE to Jerry Lawler's USWA in Memphis, I got a call from either Vince's longtime creative partner Bruce Prichard or Jim Cornette—surprisingly that's the *one thing* I can't remember!

Whichever one called me told me they had an idea for a

new character. Originally this new wrestler was going to be "hot-shotted" (pushed immediately into a program with Undertaker, with little story build). If I recall correctly, the immediate need for such a character had something to do with Leon White, aka WWE Superstar Vader, who had gotten into trouble in Kuwait.

Again, right place, right time. Then I was told the character's name: "Inferno."

"Wait, wait, wait," I thought. "You mean to tell me, after saddling me with Isaac Yankem and fake Diesel, you are going to call me Inferno?"

I *hated* it. More importantly, Bruce hated it probably even more than I did and went to bat for me to change it.

Thankfully, that worked, and we moved on to "Kane," a name Bruce has always liked. Bruce has a son named Kane. Many will recall that the original name for Undertaker was "Kane the Undertaker," which was also Bruce's idea.

Obviously, "Kane" evokes the biblical brothers Cain and Abel, and the entire idea for Kane from the beginning was that I would be Undertaker's brother. I believe that was what Vince envisioned.

Vince liked the character so much that he wanted to put me in the slot as Undertaker's next opponent. WWE brought me up to Binghamton, New York, where a show was being held, and I brought my old Doomsday/Unabomb outfit (the getup for Doomsday in Puerto Rico was basically the same as the getup for Unabomb in Smoky Mountain). I wasn't there to wrestle that night; Vince just wanted to see me and talk about the character.

I put on my old gimmicks and Vince loved it. I thought Doomsday and Unabomb, or something that looked similar, was going to be Kane!

Then I saw the sketches of my outfit. It didn't look anything like what I had envisioned. I looked more like a superhero.

I talked to Undertaker about it and laid out my vision. I told Mark I saw Kane as more like an escaped mental patient or perhaps even the maniacal hockey mask-wearing Jason Voorhees from the *Friday the 13th* horror-movie franchise.

Yet, the Kane mock-up I had been shown looked more like a comic book crusader who would fly through the skies, cape and everything. How in the world could that be Kane?

About this same time, I began to see Paul Bearer on TV talking more and more about Kane, building up my debut. I thought: "Holy cow! This is actually about to happen!" I could tell it was going to be a big deal; I felt the pressure mounting.

This had to be done right.

That's when I finally got the courage to call Vince and tell him what I thought. He said he understood where I was coming from about the look of my character. It made me feel better.

But Vince also said I was wrong about who Kane really was.

Kane was not someone from a mental institution or a mere sadist. Kane, Vince insisted, has a "scarred ego." He's a tortured soul compensating for his ugliness and emotional dysfunction by becoming a superhero. Also, he's not disfigured as much as he perceives he's disfigured. That's just another example of how insecure and unfulfilled Kane is.

After listening, I had just one thought: "Vince is a genius!"

In the end, I got the look I wanted, but the ultimate credit for creating Kane, "The Big Red Machine," goes to Vince. I know Bruce and some of the others had a hand in developing Kane, but in the end it came down to the boss and his vision.

With a better understanding by all involved of what the Kane character should look like and what his true nature would be, WWE started putting together what would become Kane's costume. At a *Monday Night Raw* in Atlantic City, New Jersey, I met with Vince, Bruce, and J.R. to don the outfit for the first time.

Everyone loved it, including me.

Vince kept stressing that the operative word with Kane was "cool."

J.R. responded, "You know what would be cool?" He then brought up shock rock singer Marilyn Manson, who at that time was at the height of his career, and noted that during performances, the singer wore one contact lens that made his eye look sinister.

So, in addition to the costume, there would be the spooky eye that would become so integral to the overall Kane character, compliments of Good Ol' J.R. and Marilyn Manson.

But we should really take a moment to talk about my mask.

The Mask

The Kane character would end up having long hair; luckily, I had grown mine long for the fake Diesel character. I hadn't cut it in forever simply because no one had ever told me to!

I would soon learn the many painful difficulties of having both long hair and a mask.

I'm not exactly sure who came up with the original leather-mask concept, but I do know we couldn't initially find anyone to make it. After being turned away by several companies, we finally found a couple in their thirties in New York City who did this kind of work.

Their main clientele? People into S&M and bondage wear. I swear.

They were the nicest people you could possibly meet and you would have never thought in a million years this was the kind of work they did.

Terry Anderson, who has been designing costumes for WWE since 1989, had made my outfit and would make all of them over the years.

Still, the mask was a special project.

The mask was not only stitched together and dyed, but it had to be molded correctly because it had creases. The couple took a mold of my face and then soaked leather in water. It was the first time I had a full head mold. They then put the leather in an oven to cure and harden to create the creases.

The mask was expensive to make, and after this first one, Terry Anderson figured out how to make all my masks.

Believe me, there were many. That was because my sweat and rough handling caused them to discolor so much that they had to be replaced every four or five months.

People often ask what happened to the old ones. I have given a few away. Bruce Prichard has one. I gave one of my masks to a little boy with a heart condition. I gave another to the Big Boss Man for charity. Today, I still have some, including the one Undertaker ripped off my head at *SummerSlam 2000* in Raleigh, North Carolina.

The most recent masks are latex. Fans often asked if I could breathe, but that was never a problem.

Once, though, I sliced myself badly under the mask, a cut caused by the force of hitting my head during a powerslam. It was the crease in the leather that did it; it had become sharp and cut me. I could see my blood dripping onto the mat. When I got backstage and took off my mask, I was like, "Great! Just great!"

The worst things about the masks were the brass rivets that connected them to the straps that held them on my head. I would always put the mask on, then pull my hair through the straps; throughout matches, the rivets would catch in my hair.

My hair tangles easily, and every time I would take off my mask it would twist and damage my hair. I used tons of conditioner in an attempt to prevent this, but it didn't help: Each time I pulled off the mask, the brass rivets would shred my hair.

My hair was long and beautiful then—and a pain to take care of!

Debut at *Badd Blood*

Starting in April 1997, WWE began building up to my debut. With Undertaker and his former manager, Paul Bearer, officially on the outs, Taker threw a fireball in Paul's face.

Later, Paul would emerge with bandages all over his face due to the attack. Bearer wanted to rejoin with Taker, and said if he didn't take him back, he would reveal Deadman's "biggest secret."

Guess who!

Bearer said that the fire that damaged his face was not unlike another fire long ago, when Undertaker was a child. Taker refused to realign with Paul.

That was when Paul Bearer vowed to bring back Undertaker's long-lost brother, Kane, to challenge Deadman!

"Yeeeessssss, YEEEEESSSSS!"

Bearer said Taker had murdered his family by setting fire to their house, a funeral home, killing everyone except Kane. The tragedy had scarred Kane mentally and physically, Bearer said, and now there would be hell to pay for Taker.

Undertaker said Paul had it backward. He said that I was a pyromaniac, that I had started the fire—and there was no way I could have possibly survived the furious blaze caused by my own hand.

Little did he know!

The weekend before *Badd Blood*, I went to the warehouse in Stamford where I put on the outfit. I then worked out as Kane and practiced the same moves Undertaker did, everything from the sit-up to the Tombstone piledriver. For those unfamiliar, the piledriver is when a wrestler holds his opponent upside down by the waist and then forcefully lowers him straight down to the mat. Taker's famous version was dubbed the Tombstone. Cornette was there helping me every step of the way. He said the cage they would be using was chain-linked, complete with a roof to prevent escape, a throw-back to the old NWA War Games matches.

This would all lead to my debut at the pay-per-view *Badd Blood* in October 1997 during the main event between Under-taker and Shawn Michaels in the very first Hell in a Cell match.

And it was a debut that almost didn't happen!

Badd Blood was to be held in St. Louis, near my home-town, so I flew in a few days early to visit with friends and family. Since I didn't bother renting a car, my old friend Mark Morton offered me a ride to the arena on the day of the show. Mark still dabbled in wrestling with some local groups, had begun a family, and was pursuing a master's degree and career in social work. I figured it would be a good chance for us to catch up. It was a great way to start my big day.

Well, I thought it was . . . until Mark arrived.

He pulled up to my parents' house in the worst beater car I had ever seen. This bucket of bolts barely looked drivable. It was awful. Apparently, his wife had taken their other car—the nice one!

In retrospect, I should never have gotten in, but I thought, "Okay, whatever," and we hit the road. About forty-five min-utes outside of St. Louis, something happened that I never would have believed had I not seen it with my own eyes.

I looked down and saw, I kid you not, smoke coming out of *the cassette player*! How does that even happen? I said, "Dude, your car is on fire!"

He looked over, shocked to see the smoke billowing out of the cassette player. Predictably, the next thing you know, there was a loud pop and the engine chugged to a halt. As the car lost power, Mark pulled off the road.

So, there we were, stuck on the side of I-70. My first thought was that this would be the shortest-lived debut in WWE history. I wouldn't even make it to the arena!

Smoke was pouring out from under the hood, but, luckily, Mark had a cell phone; he called someone else to pick me up to get me to the show.

Fortunately, even after that bizarre scare, I still arrived at the arena two hours early. Only Vince, J.R., Bruce, Cornette, and Undertaker knew I was debuting that night. At that time, before the Kane character was unveiled, I was not yet a marquee name. No one was really concerned with me or what I might be doing that night, even though I had been on the roster for some time.

Late that evening, we learned some tragic news: Brian Pillman had died the night before in Minneapolis at age thirty-five. Many knew Brian had not made his way to St. Louis for the pay-per-view. Now we were finding out why. An autopsy attributed his death to a heart attack.

Unfortunately, I had never really gotten to know Brian, and amazingly, I don't think we ever met. When he came to WWE, I was busy wrestling in Mexico or for Jerry Lawler in Memphis.

Still, it was a dark cloud that hung over that evening.

I didn't realize it at the time, but *Badd Blood* would be a day of many firsts. When we rehearsed my debut, it was the first time I heard my music, learned that I had a fireworks display, or pyro, and came up with some of Kane's most iconic gestures.

When I heard my music, I liked it immediately. It was another gem from Jim Johnston, who had created some of the most memorable themes in WWE history. It was dramatic and big, perfect for Kane. I would have different versions of my entrance music over the years, but my favorite was always 2008's "Slow Chemical" by the band Finger 11.

As Undertaker and I went over what we were going to do, we were told there needed to be a cue for the pyro. It was Taker's idea for me to put my hands up over my head and throw them down quickly to cue the flames.

The idea came from Kane simply doing the opposite of Undertaker. If Taker raised his arms to bring up the lights, I would slam my arms down to summon hellfire.

Kane was supposed to be a mirror image of Undertaker, so it was perfect. I have to give Taker a lot of credit for that idea and so many others that became integral parts of my career.

Though so many fans today associate *Badd Blood* with my debut, I thought the focus still needed to be on the match between Taker and Shawn. They were the main event. I was an added bonus.

And in the end, as memorable as it was, I didn't really do much that night!

When the lights went down and my music hit, I walked out with Paul Bearer, and Vince, on commentary, gave the iconic line "That's gotta be Kane!"

I got a huge pop from the crowd.

I ripped the cell door off its hinges, which consisted of me pantomiming shaking it so hard that it seemed locked. I actually lifted the door off its hinges, something we had rehearsed earlier in the day.

After I stared down Undertaker and lowered my arms, the flames shot up and the lights were raised. Then Taker gave me the signal to scoop him up for a Tombstone piledriver.

If you go back and watch on the WWE Network, you will notice that I turn around a few times before delivering the move to Taker. Looks pretty dramatic, right? It looked like I was parading him around the ring and building the suspense.

That wasn't what I was doing at all. I couldn't remember where the hard camera was! That is the main, fixed camera that captures most of the action during TV tapings. I was literally lost. I just wanted to make sure I was giving the Tombstone piledriver from the right angle so it looked good on TV.

After all, we didn't go through all this to make it look shoddy!

When we got backstage, everyone was happy about how the match and my debut had gone. Vince was sitting just behind the curtain in what we call Gorilla Position, which back then was just a table and not the more elaborate setup many are familiar with today. He didn't jump up and down in excitement or anything, but I could tell Vince was happy. Bruce was, too. Cornette was ecstatic.

Everyone felt like we hit a home run.

I was happy—and *relieved*.

It was so important to me that the fans reacted as they did. Even with all the high fives and excitement backstage, I couldn't help but think about the fact that I had had two failed characters before, and I couldn't afford to mess this opportunity up.

This was my shot. I couldn't miss.

After my debut, I thought, "So far, so good," and it *felt good*. Sure, I had had a big match with Bret Hart at *Summer-Slam 1995*, but I had never been invested in the Isaac Yankem character, for good or ill.

This was different. I had been nervous walking onto the stage that night in St. Louis because I was putting everything I had into Kane and the company was investing so heavily in this story line and in me.

Now that it was over, I felt more relief than elation. I had done my part and everything was good. Thank God.

But we were just getting started.

Monday Night Raw in Kansas City

The thing about sports entertainment is you never have time to breathe and pat yourself on the back. There's always a show tomorrow.

Even after any given *WrestleMania* is over, Vince never sits back and relishes the moment. He's already getting ready for next year.

So I had a great debut. Next!

That said, when we got to *Monday Night Raw* the following night, I got more feedback than I had gotten on Sunday. That was helpful and I was still feeling good.

That *Raw* in Kansas City proved to be more important than my debut had been, and The Hardy Boyz had a lot to do with it. I had met Matt and Jeff Hardy before. They were mostly unknown at this point, having come to WWE from the independent scene doing one-off matches as enhancement for our stars.

That was exactly what they were hired to do for me that night.

As Matt and Jeff were shown in the ring ready for a tag team match, my music played as Paul and I sauntered into the ring, interrupting them. I knocked Matt out of the ring and threw Jeff on top of him, and the guys really made me look strong. That toss looked good, and Matt and Jeff—who were only in their early twenties at the time—were the reason why.

That was when Paul started talking. "Ladies and gentlemen, let me present to you," he said to the audience in his hallmark high shrill, "Undertaker's little brother, Kane!"

The audience roared and the camera zoomed in on my face. My only job was to look menacing, which wasn't hard to do in that mask, with black makeup around my eyes and my Marilyn Manson contact lens.

"Look close, Undertaker!" Paul yelled in his twisted, sermonic style. "The whole world saw your face last night, when you stood, for the first time in twenty years, face-to-face with your own brother. We could all tell by the look in your eyes that you knew it was him!

"Yes, he's alive," Paul continued. "Look in his eye, Undertaker. He's missing an eye! And it's *your fault*! The twenty years of suffering, the twenty years of hiding out, is now over. And we have you to thank, Undertaker!"

The camera zoomed in close so the audience could gaze upon my disturbing-looking eye with the blue contact. Thanks, J.R.!

"Undertaker, this is your stop sign on your highway to eternity," Paul said. "Starting with these boys tonight! We are going to walk through [WWE], take each one, each wrestler, one by one and destroy them *until we beat you*!"

"You, Undertaker. That is why Kane is here," Paul declared. "Every time you look around, you're going to see your brother behind you."

At that moment, the *Raw* cameras showed a young man in the audience staring at me, his jaw gaping in seeming disbelief at what he was witnessing. Another fan held a sign in the crowd that read CAIN LIVES DEAD MAN, indicating that not only was Kane getting over with the crowd, but that my character was so new that some didn't know how to spell my name yet.

It was working. "Every time you close your eyes to go to sleep," Paul said to Undertaker, wherever he was, "you're going to remember that terrible night—the fire, oh yes, the fire."

"Undertaker, welcome to your worst nightmare!" Paul finished—and my music hit.

"This man is a monster, *a monster*!" J.R. bellowed from the announce table.

It was perfect.

Path of Destruction

When Paul said I was going to walk through WWE, picking off wrestlers one by one until I got my revenge on Undertaker, he wasn't kidding. For the next six months, that was exactly the plan, and it proved key to establishing Kane as a monster heel.

Jim Cornette told me at the time that I had the best spot in the company because I was going to destroy every babyface on the roster except Steve Austin and, of course, Undertaker.

Road Warrior Hawk. Ahmed Johnson. Flash Funk. Crush. Dude Love (another one of Mick Foley's personas, a fun-loving hippie). I demolished all of them, with Paul cutting blistering promos for every match.

Those few months were some of the absolute greatest for me as Kane. I remember appearing on a nationally televised daytime program with other WWE Superstars and being asked what my thoughts were on 1997. I replied that it was the best year ever because I had destroyed everyone!

Kane was getting over, and it was thanks in no small part to the many already established stars who had no problem getting beaten by the former Isaac Yankem and fake Diesel who was finally on his way to becoming a star in his own right.

I appreciated every single one of them, more than they know. I thank them all just as heartily and humbly today. They did an immeasurable favor for a guy who had been in the business awhile but really needed a big breakthrough.

Thanks to them, I was finally getting it.

I remember when I was working in Smoky Mountain, Al Snow once said, "You know who the most powerful man in WWE is? Barry Horowitz."

For years, Horowitz worked for WWE as an enhancement talent, meaning that his job was to make our biggest Superstars look good in the ring without any expectation of becoming more high profile himself within the company.

Al basically said that if Undertaker gave Barry a Tombstone piledriver, the most destructive move in WWE, and Horowitz sold it, everyone would buy into what just happened.

On the other hand, if Taker were to give Barry his most brutal finisher and Horowitz simply got up, brushed off his head like nothing happened, and jumped over the top rope to scurry off, everyone would think Undertaker was an incompetent fraud.

If Barry didn't do his job, no one would believe that Undertaker was a force to be reckoned with.

Al was right. Being a big star in WWE is the goal for so many, but it's the people who make the star shine who are most important.

That was what so many of my friends and colleagues did for me between October 1997 and April of the following year—and I will be eternally grateful to them for their help.

Riding with Paul Bearer

As my star rose, Paul Bearer and I started traveling together.

Since no one was supposed to know what I looked like,

I would often wear a ski mask or put a towel over my head while riding in the car with Paul, especially at night, when entering the arenas.

I'll never forget pulling into the San Diego Sports Arena, at a time when WWE was getting super hot. Steve Austin was then the biggest thing in sports entertainment—beginning to achieve a mainstream popularity not seen in our business since Hulk Hogan—and The Rock (aka Dwayne Johnson) was right on his heels, about to take off into superstardom.

That day in San Diego, under the ramp where we pulled into the arena, at least five thousand fans stood lined up to catch a glimpse of their favorite Superstar.

Think about it. That's five thousand fans just hanging around outside. The show wouldn't start for hours!

On that particular night, Paul told me he wasn't feeling well and asked me to drive. We had rented a red Cadillac, not the most inconspicuous car to carry a mysterious, masked Superstar. Paul was hunkered down next to me, looking sick.

But, as I pulled into the arena wearing a ski mask—let that scene sink in for a moment—Paul jerked to life, rolled down his window, and screamed to the thousands of waiting fans, "It's a miracle, Kane can drive! Kane can drive!"

He got me. I had to laugh.

Another time, we landed in Los Angeles for a show in Anaheim. Paul was dying to go to El Torito, a Mexican restaurant that was also in Anaheim. I needed to go to the gym and had always visited the original Gold's Gym in Venice Beach when I was in the area.

I got to the gym, but traffic afterward was so terrible—remember, we're in LA—that there was no way we were also going to be able to make it to the restaurant.

Paul was so mad he didn't talk to me for two days.

After that, we had a show in Salt Lake City and Paul still wasn't talking to me. Later that night, we went to a nice steak house with our friends Phineas I. and Henry O. Godwinn, the ring names for a WWE tag team. I picked up the check.

Paul thought that was the greatest thing ever and the El Torito incident was forgotten.

During that time, we often traveled with Scotty Taylor, aka Scotty 2 Hotty of the soon-to-be-popular tag team Too Cool. Paul and I would share driving duties and Scotty—who wasn't old enough to rent a car—would sit in the back by himself.

Paul was one of the sweetest men I have ever known. Unfortunately, he passed away in 2013 at age fifty-eight. It was an honor to induct him into the WWE Hall of Fame the following year.

Though times could be tough, Paul had a heart of gold. He took care of everything. In WWE, the company booked your flights, but talent had to take care of the rest, including hotels and car rentals.

Paul booked all of it. He took care of us. I'll never forget it.

And I will never forget my friend, who had as much to do with the success of Kane as anyone.

Survivor Series in Montreal (Yes, That One)

My first actual match as Kane—as opposed to just showing up everywhere and annihilating everyone in my path—was with Mankind at *Survivor Series 1997.*

Yes, at the infamous "Montreal Screwjob" pay-per-view. We'll get to that.

Mick Foley as Dude Love had been one of Kane's many victims in recent months, but here Mick was returning as his much darker Mankind character.

What I remember most about the match, even more than winning, was how we got to the finish. I threw Mankind off the top turnbuckle, slamming him hard onto the outside floor. It was brutal. Mick had asked me to do it beforehand.

He was doing crazy stuff long before the famous fall from the top of Hell in a Cell the following year at the hands of Undertaker. Mick was always trying to outdo himself with bigger and more spectacular stunts. Our match that night was no exception.

Vince didn't want Kane and Undertaker on the same show, so Mark didn't have a match that night.

But Bret Hart and Shawn Michaels did.

Like most of the locker room, Paul and I had absolutely no idea what was about to go down.

For those unfamiliar with this piece of sports entertainment lore, Bret was leaving WWE to join Ted Turner's rival World Championship Wrestling (WCW), which had been beating WWE in television ratings. (Despite WWE's exploding popularity during this time, we would not surpass WCW in the ratings for another five months.)

This colossal, years-long battle between these two sports entertainment powerhouses is remembered today as the Monday Night War.

As the Canadian hero, Bret did not want to lose the title in his home country. So that night, Vince, in what would end up becoming the origin of his Mr. McMahon character, called for the bell prematurely, thereby awarding Shawn the victory, even though Bret had never submitted.

When the hastened finish came, with Shawn putting Bret in Bret's own signature submission hold, called the Sharpshooter, and referee Earl Hebner yelling, "Ring the bell!" we still didn't know what to think. Bret was going nuts, of course. Shawn had left with the WWE Championship.

Among the many of us who were watching backstage, the general feeling was, "What the heck was that? Was it part of the story line? Did Bret actually get screwed?"

We didn't really know what to think.

As Paul and I headed to our car, we saw Earl and his brother, Dave Hebner, in a big hurry to get out of there. They hadn't even bothered changing their clothes, which was unusual.

I ended up talking to Mick about it backstage. He was upset and said he was going to quit. In the hotel room later, Mick got a call from Vince and *hung up on him*! Mick would not take Vince's call.

I was like, "Dude, what are you doing?" I told him he should calm down and really think this through.

Mick did not show up for TV the next day. I also don't remember Davey Boy Smith or Owen Hart being at that television taping.

I remember we were in some little town outside Montreal and Vince came walking in with a black eye. He explained his side of things. He said he had tried to work with Bret the best he could, but his World Champion still refused to drop the title in Canada, despite the fact that he was going to WCW.

Though it's complicated, I ultimately side with Vince in his decision that night.

Many look at the Monday Night War as an awesome time in the sports entertainment business. It was. It was also a very stressful time. People were afraid for their jobs.

In the end, this is still a business. Vince did what was right for business.

As I understand it, after WCW offered Bret a big-money contract, Vince countered with his own attractive, long-term deal. Vince should probably have never countered. He should have let Bret go to WCW right then and there.

Because later, when Vince told Bret he wanted out of their contract and encouraged him to see if he could still make some good money with WCW, it was just too convoluted.

But the real reason Vince was ultimately right had nothing to do with titles, or his ego, or how he felt about Bret, or Shawn, or any of the other things people have speculated about over the last two decades.

Vince had to protect his product because he had to protect *us*. As much as himself, his company, and his family, he was looking out for everyone on his roster and their families.

We were in an all-out war with another major pro-wrestling company, and it was highly likely one side was eventually going to win.

One eventually did.

On a lighter note, it was during WWE's jaunt through Canada that winter that I began doing the head-tilt gimmick that would become an enduring part of the Kane character. Ottawa was the first place I tried it, tilting my head slightly to the side in an almost understated way, while looking at my opponent or into the camera. It always got a great reaction. Bruce Prichard, who had been so instrumental in my character's initial development, said I got more emotion from the crowd with that one simple move than I could with a fiery promo.

Over the years, many have assumed the head tilt must have come from some deep, dark place in Kane's demonic mind.

Nope. It came from my St. Bernard, Annie. She would always tilt her head when I said her name.

Tormenting Deadman

After my rivalry with Mankind, I moved on to Vader. Vader was the real deal, a 350-pounder who could do moonsaults, a flipping move off the turnbuckle normally reserved for cruiserweights. No one had ever seen anything like him.

When wrestlers start a match, they typically start with the light stuff and move into heavier moves as things progress.

Not Leon, or at least not with me. Every match, he would begin by punching me in the face really hard. Then I would legit punch him back in the face really hard. We did that every night. Pay-per-views, television tapings, house shows, it didn't matter.

It was always like he gave me that first punch to see what I was going to do, while I was thinking, "Why do we have to do this every time?"

Leon was another good guy who helped forge Kane's path. I'm sorry that he's not still with us today. Sadly, he died in June 2018 after a long struggle with heart problems.

The sole purpose of my program with Vader was to continue building me up before my eventual showdown with Undertaker. But before that would happen, Taker and I still had plenty of storytelling to do.

During this time I was laying waste to the biggest babyfaces on the roster, and I would interrupt Undertaker during his matches and promos. But we never touched. This was important; it built anticipation.

It was all about intimidation and mind games. The idea was that we would constantly interact, but never really fight.

A lot of these angles had to do with Taker refusing to fight me, his estranged little brother. At a December *Raw* in 1997, Paul and I interrupted Undertaker yet again. I slapped Undertaker. I tried to slap him again, but he blocked me. Instead of retaliating, he just walked to the back.

It was a great angle, but it bothered me. Even though the story line was going really well and helping us both, I didn't feel right going out there and just slapping Undertaker. Who does that? Taker is the most respected person in the WWE locker room, and you can put me at the top of his list of admirers.

Before we went out to the ring that night, I walked up to Taker and told him he needed to slap me right there. He was like "Are you serious?" He insisted it wasn't a big deal.

I said it was to me. So, he slapped me hard. *Really hard.*

My immediate thought was "Why did I ask him to slap me?" And then, "I'm going to slap the snot out of him next time we're out there!"

What's that old saying about being careful what you wish for?

In the ring and in promos, everything I did was done with the intention of goading Taker into fighting me. We did a segment on *Raw* where Taker stood in the ring threatening me in an interview; then Paul and I popped up on the TitanTron. We were standing in the "graveyard" where Undertaker's "parents," and mine, were "buried."

Paul reminded Taker in every interview that it was his fault they had perished in the house fire he allegedly started, and that Undertaker had "murdered" his own parents.

Paul then handed me a sledgehammer and I smashed the two headstones before us. "That's his own mother and father's gravesite!" J.R. screamed to the *Raw* audience. "He's desecrating his own parents' grave!"

Then I set the graves on fire. Undertaker looked on, enraged but motionless and silent. Then *Raw* went dark and bled into a commercial break.

It was another perfect chapter in our ongoing saga. But I remember it for other reasons.

Some people think WWE Superstars lead glamorous and exciting lives. In many ways, that's true. But during the day-to-day routine, more often than not, it doesn't feel that way.

The day of the graveyard scene on *Raw*, Paul and I had awakened at 5 a.m. in Syracuse, New York, where the show was happening, to catch a flight to New York City, and then drive to Stamford, Connecticut, to shoot the segment.

Yes, for those unaware, Undertaker's "parents," and mine, were "buried" at the TV studios of WWE headquarters.

After we finished, we flew back to Syracuse because Paul and I were booked to walk out during the dark match (in wrestling parlance, an untelevised match) after *Raw* went off the air that night.

WWE Superstars' schedules are grueling. Sometimes I don't know how we did it.

One *Raw* during this time has always stuck out in my mind: Paul and I were shown backstage wheeling around a dirty casket. Paul was a huge country music fan—probably the biggest George Jones fan on earth—and so, appropriately, the camera showed him singing the Randy Travis hit "Diggin' Up Bones" as he pushed a deteriorated carcass toward the main stage.

I wonder if non-WWE fans flipping through the channels that night came across this scene and thought, "What in the world is on my TV?"

But that was the tame part. Soon, we would reveal that these were the caskets of our "parents," Taker's and mine, which Paul and I had just dug up twenty years after they had been buried. I set my father's casket on fire, and when an angry Undertaker rushed me, I Chokeslammed him through our mother's casket. Close-up shots showed a decimated Taker lying amid the broken wood; others showed our mother's "bones"; worms could be seen crawling through the dirt and other remains.

Again, it was classic Kane terrorizing Undertaker. High-level storytelling. Anyone unfamiliar with sports entertainment would have thought we were absolutely nuts.

The WWE Universe ate it up.

I could write an entire chapter on everyone I Chokeslammed over the years, even leaving out actual Superstars. I Chokeslammed a priest, the Easter Bunny, and even the Phoenix Suns' mascot, a gorilla.

I remember Paul telling me that beating up a guy in a gorilla costume was "too much haha." Paul felt it was a comedy skit that would hurt Kane's dark persona. I was, like, "Am I really doing this?" I talked to Bruce Prichard and he said it was definitely happening.

The hoped-for payoff for the Phoenix Suns' gorilla spot was that it would be replayed on ESPN's *SportsCenter*. That was a gamble because some of the producers at ESPN didn't like WWE, even though others were huge fans.

That night, the producers must have been fans because *SportsCenter* showed me Chokeslamming the Suns' gorilla.

Then there was Pete Rose.

Pete Rose Had It Coming

I am certain that if Pete Rose hadn't pursued a career in baseball, he would have been a great wrestling heel.

One of Kane's most iconic moments occurred in 1998 at *WrestleMania XIV* in Boston, prior to my match with Undertaker, when I delivered a patented Tombstone piledriver to the guest ring announcer—Major League Baseball's all-time hit king, Pete Rose.

I learned about the bit with Rose the day of the show. That often happens in WWE. Some things are planned for months, but so much of the good stuff is the result of last-second inspiration.

Pete and I went over the Tombstone, but I didn't know what he was going to say when introducing me or any other details. I'm glad I didn't because Pete Rose was pure magic on the microphone and my reactions to his banter must have been persuasive because they were authentic.

Being a St. Louis Cardinals baseball fan, I reserve a dark corner of my heart for hatred of the New York Mets. When I was growing up, the phrase "The Mets are pond scum" had crept into the patois of Cardinals fans.

We didn't appreciate Pete Rose much, either. "Charlie Hustle" was one of those guys you loved when he played for your team, but you loved to hate him when he played for your opponent's.

In 1986, the World Series featured the Mets versus the Boston Red Sox. In the tenth inning of Game Six, Red Sox great Bill Buckner committed one of the most famous errors in baseball history, allowing the Mets to win the game and eventually the series.

Twelve years later, Pete Rose was standing in a WWE ring in the middle of the Boston's Fleet Center with a microphone in his hand.

"I left some tickets for Bill Buckner, but he couldn't bend over to pick 'em up," Pete said, finishing with a gratuitous, "How 'bout it?"

The crowd booed Rose out of the building. I arrived in the ring with Paul Bearer, walked up to Rose, grabbed him by the throat, and hoisted him onto my shoulder before dropping him on his head.

The crowd went crazy as Rose was taken out of the ring and to the back on a stretcher.

My next encounter with Rose was in Philadelphia the following year, at *WrestleMania XV*. As I made my way to the ring for my match against Triple H, the world-famous San Diego Chicken made its *WrestleMania* debut, attacking me from behind. I grabbed the mascot and pulled off its head, revealing a stunned and defeated "Hit King."

Same result: I dropped Rose on his head. The only difference was this time he was wearing a chicken outfit instead of a tuxedo.

Next year was *WrestleMania 2000* in Anaheim, California. I had been involved in a fierce rivalry with my former tag team partner, X-Pac, leading to a tag match between X-Pac and his D-Generation X stablemate, Road Dogg, against Rikishi and me.

Rikishi was a unique character, a cross between a sumo wrestler and a hip-hop artist. During that time, he was always joined in the ring after a match by his associates, the tag team Too Cool—Scotty 2 Hotty and Grandmaster Sexay. The house lights would dim and be replaced with disco balls. The music hit, and the three of them would delight the audience with their dance routine.

For a reason known only to the wrestling gods, after our tag match at *WrestleMania 2000,* during which we beat X-Pac and Road Dogg, the San Diego Chicken suddenly appeared in the ring to join Rikishi and Too Cool in their postmatch celebration.

Because it was obvious that Pete Rose was going back to the same ill-fated tricks, I snatched that Chicken by his beak!

But the man in the chicken suit was not Rose. The ruse worked. As I struggled to unmask the Chicken, Rose slid in the ring behind me armed with a baseball bat.

Throughout his career, Rose had been known as a singles hitter, but that night he was winding up for a home run. Luckily, Rikishi grabbed the bat out of Rose's hands. I followed with a Chokeslam. Rikishi finished off the Hit King with his patented "Stink Face."

The Stink Face is what Rikishi gave WWE Superstars when they found themselves slumped down on the mat with their backs and heads against the second turnbuckle. Rikishi would stick his bulbous derriere right in their faces, traumatizing them.

In my experience, Pete Rose was always a trouper, a show-man, and a professional. He understood WWE is entertainment and wanted to put on a good show, even when he was the butt of the joke.

After our encounter at *WrestleMania 2000*, Pete caught up to me backstage. He handed me the bat he had brought to the ring. It was signed "Pete Rose, Hit King #4256." That bat is one of my most prized possessions.

In 2004, I had the honor of inducting Pete Rose into the Celebrity Wing of the WWE Hall of Fame. While the debate rages on about whether he belongs in baseball's Hall of Fame, Rose's iconic moments at *WrestleMania* assured him a place in WWE's.

And to all those Cardinals baseball fans who loved to hate Pete, those Tombstones were for you!

Kane and Undertaker Get Superpowers

They needed to find different ways for Taker and me to continue our rivalry until our eventual *WrestleMania* showdown, while keeping us apart physically, or at least not beating each other up for too long on any given segment.

So they decided to give us superpowers.

One night on *Raw*, Paul and I entered the ring to intimidate Undertaker and everyone else by revealing my secret powers. "Show them what you can do!" Paul commanded.

I shot lightning bolts toward Jim Ross and Michael Cole at the announce table. "How do you like that, leeches of the night!?" Paul screamed.

"That damn spotlight has been in my eyes all night, Kane," Paul said to me, pointing at the lighting rig. "Kill it!" he demanded. I moved my arm and fist, which made the spotlight explode and the crewmember running it slump over in his perch high above the arena.

Paul then told me, basically, to do whatever I wanted to do with my powers. So, I shot lightning through my hands at a crew member wandering near the bottom of the entrance ramp. He ran backstage, engulfed in flames.

"Burn, baby, burn!" Paul cackled.

While the audience in the arena saw the explosions and the fire, no one in attendance could see the lightning bolts. That spectacle was just for the audience at home. Remember, this was 1997. Still, WWE's production expertise was ahead of its time, and we could superimpose lightning onto the screen in real time.

It was amazing. WWE was second to none in its technological capabilities compared to most others in television.

Once, when visiting our satellite truck, team members told me that their editing and rendering capabilities far surpassed those of CNN. They said that we could do things even major cable news outlets couldn't do at the time.

And, let's face it, no other characters in WWE could have pulled off possessing such fantastical powers except The Big Red Machine and Deadman. This was our own, unique territory, and we exploited it to create some of the most memorable moments of the Attitude Era.

It simply wouldn't have worked with anyone else.

The Last *Raw* Before *Royal Rumble*, in State College, Pennsylvania

On the *Monday Night Raw* prior to *Royal Rumble 1998*, Shawn Michaels was advertised as having a big announcement.

He invited Kane to join D-Generation X.

"Everybody saw last week," Shawn began his invitation to me on *Raw*, "Paul Bearer and Kane have split ways [we had had a minor tiff], and Kane has wandered out into the world all alone. D-Generation X would be glad to stand here, open arms, like the family Kane never had and accept him into our family of D-Generation X."

"Ladies and gentlemen, the newest member of D-Generation X—Kane!" Shawn announced, pointing to the entrance curtain.

That was when Undertaker's music hit.

After his entrance, Taker entered the ring surrounded by DX and told Shawn point-blank, "Now Michaels, I would appreciate it if you left my family out of this. This has nothing to do with my little brother Kane."

Now let's make one thing clear: Taker had a point here. While I had been terrorizing my older brother for months, this did not mean Kane was necessarily a fan of D-Generation X. The Big Red Machine wasn't really a big fan of anyone except maybe Paul Bearer and, obviously, even that was questionable.

"If I was you," Taker said to Shawn, "I'd be worried about the *Royal Rumble*, the WWE Title, and Undertaker punching about a six-inch hole right in the middle of your forehead."

Undertaker grabbed Shawn by the neck. Then he let him go to turn around and grab Chyna by the neck. This was really one of the first times Chyna was made to look vulnerable.

Triple H then cracked a crutch across Undertaker's back and ran away as HBK (Shawn Michaels, aka Heartbreak Kid, or HBK) surprised Undertaker with his trademark Superkick to the chin. Taker was laid out as Shawn kept walloping him with the crutch, and D-Generation X all ganged up on Deadman.

That's when the chants started. *"We want Kane! We want Kane!"* I could hear the crowd backstage and immediately got goose bumps. Fifteen thousand people. They kept getting louder. I thought to myself, echoing a chant more popular in today's WWE, *"This is awesome!"*

Then the lights went down, my music hit, and I walked through the curtain.

The crowd erupted. It was time to take care of business.

"He'll walk right through hell! He's Kane!" J.R. screamed. "The question is, is he coming to assist DX or to *dismantle* them?" Jerry Lawler kept saying he was sure I was there to help D-Generation X and maybe even join them as a new member.

At the time, D-Generation X's members included Shawn, Triple H, and Chyna.

But no, I didn't want to join them.

Instead, I snatched Shawn by the hair to stop him from punching Taker, which he had done repeatedly. The audience went bonkers. Triple H hit me in the back with his crutch to draw me away from destroying Shawn. Then Hunter ran like a coward. All of DX did.

"Nobody wants any part of Kane," J.R. yelled. "Kane has come to help his brother!"

I chased D-Generation X to the back and turned around at the top of the ramp to stare at Taker, who was still stumbling around the ring due to the beatdown he had just received. He finally gathered his wits and stopped dead in his tracks. He stared right back at me.

I extended my hand from a distance, the camera catching the perfect side profile of The Big Red Machine, who appeared to be presenting a peace offering to The Deadman.

The audience was on their feet. They loved every minute of it.

"Kane is apparently extending his hand in some sort of bond of friendship," J.R. said. "And Undertaker is returning it!"

Jim said this as Taker dropped to one knee and threw his head back. His eyes rolled backward into his skull as he extended his hand right back at me.

"Oh, what a moment!" J.R. wailed. "Undertaker seemed as if he had a smile on his face!"

Note: Undertaker never has a smile on his face. This was more like mafia members kissing the Godfather's ring. The ring of death!

The Brothers of Destruction would not come until later, but we planted the seed for the first time that night. It was magic.

And the WWE Universe couldn't wait.

Royal Rumble in San Antonio

The *Royal Rumble* is one of the most popular WWE pay-per-views not only because of the Rumble itself, which is always exciting, but because it has long been the most crucial event in setting up or cementing story lines that will come to a grand finale at *WrestleMania*.

January 1998 was no different. Stone Cold Steve Austin would win the Rumble that year by throwing out The Rock as his last competitor in the ring, but the main event was the WWE Champion Shawn Michaels vs. Undertaker in a Casket Match.

And you know that, just as in their inaugural Hell in a Cell match three months prior, Kane was going to be a big part of this show, too.

Shawn and Taker had a great match, as usual, one that ended with HBK keeping the WWE Title because D-Generation X hit the ring to gang up on Undertaker.

The last time Undertaker lost a Casket Match—*his trademark match*—had been four years prior against Yokozuna at *Royal Rumble 1994*. Now, he was being beat down gang style by a bunch of degenerates.

It was time for Kane to "break it down."

My music hit, Kane's fiery sonic boom pierced the arena, my flames burst upward, and I rolled into the ring like a tank, ready to take out every last member of D-Generation X.

Kane had come to save Undertaker! "There he is!" shouted J.R. "This unholy alliance of these brothers of the night! Kane is coming to help his brother!"

Sorry, J.R. Not happening!

A dazed Taker staggered before me and I elbowed him hard in the face. "Come on!" J.R. screamed. "No, dammit!"

I kept pounding away on Undertaker.

"Kane is assaulting his brother!" J.R. said, with torturous disappointment.

Paul Bearer started walking down. I threw Taker into the casket, and DX's Shawn and Hunter slammed the door shut.

That was how Shawn, technically, won the match and kept his WWE Title.

Paul and I began putting padlocks on the casket, making sure there was no way Undertaker could escape. We began rolling an "entombed" Taker up the entrance ramp. I pulled out an ax and started chopping away at the top of the casket, piercing it while Undertaker was still lying inside it.

It was a brutal spectacle. "This is hideous!" J.R. yelled. "This is nothing but carnage!"

Then I doused the entire casket in gasoline; Paul lit the match; and we both set Undertaker ablaze while he was still trapped inside.

I dropped down to one knee, just like Undertaker, and extended my hand upward, summoning hell, as the flames engulfed the casket.

"The casket is on fire!" J.R. cried out. "Undertaker is in the casket!"

No one saw Undertaker again until right before *Wrestle-Mania*, three months later.

Kane vs. Undertaker at *WrestleMania XIV*

"*Kane!*" Undertaker thundered on *Monday Night Raw* two weeks before what would prove to be the biggest match of my career to date.

"At *WrestleMania XIV*, I will strike down upon thee with anger and furious vengeance!" Taker said, standing on top of the TitanTron and looking down on me in the ring. "I will deliver you to the fiery pits of eternal damnation.

"You will know my name as the Lord of Darkness!" Taker continued. "Little brother, I've felt your wrath. Now you're gonna feel mine!

"It's too late to turn back," Taker said. "The only thing that you can do now is *rest in peace*!"

With that, a bolt of lightning came from the sky (for home viewers at least), setting a statue of me on fire.

Undertaker had burned Kane in effigy.

Despite the cool buildup to *WrestleMania*, a lot of it was a blur to me until the event.

What I do remember vividly is constantly thinking about how far I had come. I had gone from being an evil dentist relegated mostly to the midcard to a star in one of the most high-profile matches at *WrestleMania* that year. We were on the same card with Shawn Michaels vs. Stone Cold Steve Austin for the WWE Championship with Mike Tyson as the Special Guest Enforcer.

It doesn't get any bigger than that.

We were in Boston and I remember taking a carriage ride the night before with Crystal and just sort of soaking it all in.

On the day of *WrestleMania*, most of the performers get there early and rehearsed. Undertaker and I didn't do that.

The night before, I went to Taker's hotel room and we went over the match. He wanted to lay it out like the famous Muhammad Ali vs. George Foreman "rope-a-dope" match at the "Rumble in the Jungle" in Kinshasa, Zaire, in 1974. Many years later, Foreman famously laughed about the contest, saying that he had been the "dope" because Ali had caused Foreman to exhaust himself by throwing barrages of ineffective punches so that he was virtually defenseless by the time Ali moved in for the knockout punch.

I dominated Taker for the majority of the match. I even pinned Mark and, right before the three count, jerked him up by his hair to stop him from being beaten. One of Taker's more memorable comeback attempts during my onslaught was when he went flying over the top and came crashing down on the announce table, flattening it. I took advantage of that, too.

I was taking him apart, piece by piece, for almost the entire match. Like Ali and Foreman, it was a massacre—until it wasn't.

Now, at this point, no one had kicked out of Undertaker's Tombstone piledriver (except maybe Hulk Hogan, but as far as the audience that night was concerned, it had never been done).

As Undertaker began his comeback, J.R. said, "Maybe the rope-a-dope has taken its toll on Kane!" Nice one, J.R. When he laid me out with the Tombstone and I kicked out, the crowd was shocked. No one believed it.

"*Oh Gawd!*" J.R. screamed. "Nobody's ever done that! Nobody's ever kicked out of The Undertaker's Tombstone!"

After I did a ramrod straight sit-up, Deadman style, and walked right back almost zombie-like into a waiting Taker, I got another Tombstone.

"Well this has got to be it!" J.R. screamed. "Kane kicked out! Good Lord!" No one could believe it. The little brother of Undertaker had not only survived the Tombstone piledriver but had done so twice!

After I popped out of the second Tombstone, Paul Bearer was on the outside acting like he was having a heart attack, and the audience was on their feet, not sure of what might come next. We had taken the match into uncharted territory, which had been the idea all along.

Taker clotheslined me from the top turnbuckle, from which I also sat up almost immediately, again just like Undertaker would. "Look at Kane sit right up!" J.R. said. "It's amazing!"

That's when he delivered the third Tombstone piledriver. The crowd watched the 1-2-3, many no doubt expecting me to pop my shoulder up again. I popped out, but it was after the three count was over. So close.

I had finally lost, but barely.

After I was pinned, Bearer threw a steel chair into the ring and tried to get some licks in on Taker before Bearer was pushed to the ground. Then I delivered a postmatch

Tombstone to Taker on the steel chair. "I've seen war on small countries with less intensity than this!" J.R. yelled.

Even in my defeat, Kane was still being portrayed as an unstoppable force. That was all Undertaker and his influence. He didn't have to do that. He could have buried me at *WrestleMania* if he had wanted to. After all, that was where story lines are supposed to reach their ultimate climax and conclusion.

But Taker was wise enough to know that, while he had to win the match, it would be smart business to get as much mileage out of the Kane character as possible.

Which would lead to one of the craziest matches I've ever had.

The First Inferno Match

After *WrestleMania*, the Undertaker–Kane rivalry was so hot that WWE decided to literally turn up the heat with the first ever "Inferno Match," which was set to take place at *Unforgiven 1998*.

The idea was that flames would somehow engulf the ring, but instead of the ropes being on fire, an apparatus surrounding the ring would shoot flames into the air.

The pay-per-view event would take place in Greensboro, North Carolina, but we had a show the night before, in Fayetteville. The plan was for Paul and me to fly into Greensboro, drive nearly one hundred miles to Fayetteville and then back to Greensboro to rehearse the match.

WWE had a car take us, and it was an experience I will never forget. As Paul and I waited, up pulled a limousine. I use the term loosely. It was all beat up; the windows didn't work; when we went to a drive-thru to get something to eat, we had to open the doors to get our food.

The trip was in progress as Paul and I fell asleep, and we woke up just as we were pulling into the Fayetteville arena.

But there was just one problem. We weren't in Fayetteville. The driver had gone the wrong way!

Remember, we had no GPS or cell phones in those days. Paul called the office from a gas station pay phone. Now, instead of being just two hours from Fayetteville, we were four hours away. The office said we still had to go to Fayetteville because Undertaker and other stars who had been advertised for the event would not be appearing.

My match in Fayetteville was against Vader, and it was one of the quickest matches I ever had.

Here's how it went down: Paul and I drove the four hours back to Greensboro and then on another two hours to Fayetteville. I was still dressing in the car when we pulled up to the arena at 10:30 p.m. I jumped out of the car and immediately began my match with Vader. We fought to the ring, into the ring, out of the ring, and then back to the locker room. I jumped right back into the car to head to Greensboro. I might have been in the arena five minutes, and I don't think Paul even got out of the car.

Now we were driving back to Greensboro and I was changing in the car again. Then, about 1 a.m., after all our rushing around, we found out there would be no rehearsal that night because it was too late.

One day in the life of a WWE Superstar!

The next day, we had the actual rehearsal for the Inferno Match. I'll never forget that, either.

As we went over the match, the stunt crew was explaining to me how my arm was going to catch fire that night. We would use a special suit designed specifically for that match.

The arm of my costume was removable, fastened on with Velcro. For the finish, I would be knocked out of the ring; then Vader would come down to fight me, then Undertaker would jump on both of us.

This would leave me lying on the ground at ringside, which was key.

A band had performed on the pay-per-view earlier. Taker chased Paul Bearer to the top of the entrance ramp, where the band equipment was, and began mauling him, smashing him with a bass drum. That spot looked really cool.

But what Paul and Taker were really doing was distracting the audience away from me. During their melee, I had rolled under the ring to prepare the burn stunt.

I climbed under the ring until it covered my torso. Then I pulled off the suit's sleeve and members of the production crew helped me replace it with one made of flame-retardant material. Then they applied cooling gel with an accelerant that burned at a low temperature. Keep in mind that the "low temperature" was still a couple hundred degrees.

After he finished beating up Paul with the band's drum set, cutting him on his head, Undertaker came back to take care of me.

Undertaker knocked me into the flame at ringside and, while I was pantomiming my gimmicked arm going into the flames, my other arm touched the burner. It was like touching a hot stove!

As my arm caught fire, I had to remember everything they had told me to do: I had to keep my arms away from my face and make sure my face was turned away so I did not inhale the flames. As I ran up the ramp at the end of the match, it was important that the flames trailed me, or the rest of my suit could catch fire. It was unnerving.

The crew had said that the moment I felt any tingling or any kind of heat at all, I needed to cue them by falling down so they could spray me with fire extinguishers. They made one thing clear: My failure to follow these instructions could result in my being badly burned.

So, on top of the pressure of having to perform for thousands of spectators in the arena and for millions more who were watching on pay-per-view, I had to worry about avoiding third-degree burns!

Luckily, the match unfolded as planned, and at the end I ran to the back with my arm ablaze. It was quite a spectacle, which was the entire idea.

Undertaker had won the match by setting his little brother on fire.

In my current role as mayor, people often ask me, "What's harder, politics or WWE?"

That night, it was WWE, for sure! Although I've taken some heat in politics, I have *never* burned myself to a crisp as I almost did at *Unforgiven*!

In terms of action, this was one of the best matches we had. But, in terms of psychology, it was hard to pull off.

The winner of the match did so by putting his opponent in the fire. But, although the stunt crew had coated both of us with flame-retardant chemicals, which was especially important for two guys with long—and flammable—hair, it was so hot when we approached the flames that neither of us got close enough to look like we were in any real danger.

So, in addition to trying to have a quality match, each of us faced a significant element of physical risk. We were literally trying not to get burned alive. It was a unique match, unlike any other in WWE history.

But it wasn't just the match that I remember vividly. One of the things I remember most that day happened at rehearsal. The stunt crew WWE brought in was from Hollywood; they were professionals responsible for creating some of the most exciting scenes in our favorite movies.

I was talking with some of the crew in the parking lot outside the Greensboro Coliseum, and one guy asked, "So, you guys are going to do this real-time tonight?" I said yes. He said, "A stunt like this [in Hollywood] would usually take us about a week to set up!"

How comforting!

WWE is unlike any other business. When we're in the ring performing, we're not always thinking about just the match. We're thinking about the promo afterward, where the story might go, and how we arrived at this point.

Some of us are thinking about how to not get burned to a crisp!

Professional wrestling is a sport, but it's unlike any other sport in the world. If you play football or basketball or any other professional sport, your mind is focused solely on the game. That's what you're expected to concentrate on. In WWE, our minds could be on a million things in addition to the match we're having.

Wrestling and acting can be contrasted the same way. Professional Hollywood actors rehearse scenes and might do multiple takes before moving on to the next one. If they need dialogue in a fight scene, they can shoot it separately. It can all be edited or spliced together later.

Wrestling is not like that. One second you're talking and the next you're fighting. Maybe you're doing both simultaneously. You constantly have to be mentally prepared to multitask in this unique, hybrid business of acting and athletics.

All of these roles—athlete, actor, even stuntman—were in play during our Inferno Match. That night, we had to do something neither Undertaker nor I had ever done before, all in one long shot, without it looking cheesy, and without either of us getting hurt.

And it had to be good.

In the end, we were both proud of what we had accomplished that night.

I do remember, during a surreal moment in the match, I looked down at my arm and thought, "Wow, I'm on fire."

Only in WWE.

Kane vs. Stone Cold Steve Austin at *King of the Ring*

After *Unforgiven*, I was still in the mix with all the top stars in the company, including Undertaker and Mick Foley, but my next pay-per-view match would be against the biggest WWE Superstar of them all: Stone Cold Steve Austin.

At that time, there was no one in sports entertainment more popular—anywhere in the world—than Austin. His rivalry with McMahon had taken the industry to heights no one could have predicted just a few years earlier. His signature 3:16 T-shirts, which paraphrased a quotation of John 3:16 from the Bible to say AUSTIN 3:16 SAYS I JUST WHIPPED YOUR ASS!!!, were outselling Michael Jordan's and NASCAR's. Steve had become a mainstream pop-culture icon.

And that summer, I was right in the middle of it.

At *King of the Ring*, Steve and I were to engage in a First Blood Match for the WWE Championship. The first person to bleed would lose the match. Obviously, as the heel in that match, my suit and mask would give me a clear advantage.

But, before we got there, Austin had to accept my challenge. That would happen in Austin, Texas, on the *Raw* before the pay-per-view.

"I've bled before; I ain't afraid to bleed again," Austin said in the middle of the ring that night, thus accepting the stipulation. Ausin made it clear, however, that with the title on the line, the match was going to be a war.

The crowd went nuts.

"Let me tell you something," Steve continued. "You say that if you don't win the WWE Title, you'll set yourself on fire. I'll tell you something right now. You can bet your bottom dollar that Stone Cold Steve Austin is gonna bring all the marshmallows, all the hot dogs, and all the beer!"

The crowd roared again.

"It doesn't matter to me," Austin said. "You can be the human campfire and I'll sit there and watch you burn all day long, and if you start to go out, you can rest assured that ol' Stone Cold will be there to throw another log on the fire!"

The audience went wild—and that's when my explosions went off, flames shot up, and I walked to the stage.

Austin and I stared each other down. I tilted my head. He did not flinch.

Then, I raised my arms, and BAM! Fake blood poured down all over Steve's head. It was just like the famous scene from the movie *Carrie*, which was the idea. Austin was wearing a bright white 3:16 baseball shirt for dramatic effect. The world title in his hand was drenched.

Kane had started using a voice box to speak during this rivalry. As a shocked and "blood"-soaked Austin looked at me, I put my voice box up to my neck and spoke.

"Austin, this Sunday the blood on you will be for real," I said, in a creepy electronic vibrato. The crowd went silent for a moment, digesting what had just happened. Then they erupted, knowing that Austin would get his payback at *King of the Ring*.

We had the audience. It was perfect.

Well, almost. With the voice box, it was hard for me to find the right balance between using my actual voice, where you could understand me on mic, yet still retain the vibrato effect that made me sound spooky and weird.

Just before this segment, before the first time we used the voice gimmick in a show, Jim Cornette found me and asked, "Did you rehearse the voice box?" I said no. Cornette was like, "Oh man, someone's going to be in trouble." He said we were supposed to rehearse because no one had any idea how the voice box would sound on the mic.

When I got backstage that night, we had to rerecord the audio so the fans at home could understand what I had said. Our segment ended *Raw*.

It was the perfect lead-in to Kane and Austin's match, *King of the Ring*. Every fan remembers *King of the Ring 1998*, right? Of course you do. It was the night Mankind fought Undertaker in Hell in a Cell.

I'm still hot at Mick Foley after all these years because by the end of the night I won my first WWE Championship, but all anyone cared about was him falling off the cell.

I still tell Mick I will never forgive him.

Mick and Taker not only set the tone for the whole night, but almost (and unintentionally) put a major kink in my match with Austin.

We were all backstage at Gorilla Position—the spot behind the curtain where members of the production team sit—watching Hell in a Cell. Today, it is common knowledge among fans that Taker's move—the one that threw Mick off the cell—was planned. However, when he got Chokeslammed through the top of the cell, that was not planned. The cage was not supposed to give, but it did. That surprised everyone, especially Mick. It was the most brutal bump Mankind took all night, more so than the one he got by being thrown off the top of the cell.

We honestly didn't know if Mick was going to get back up. But, of course, being the "Hardcore Legend," he did. Watching the monitor, I was like "Oh my God! Mick's a buddy of mine. Thank goodness he's alive!"

As Mick miraculously carried on with the match, Vince looked at me. He didn't look at anyone else standing around watching the monitor, just me. I can tell you that is not a comfortable feeling.

Think about it: I'm not even a year into the Kane character; I'm wrestling the hottest commodity since Hulk Hogan, and the boss of the company is staring me down in this perilous moment.

Vince looked at me and said, "If Mick can't go back out there, you're going to have to figure out what to do in your match." Mankind was scheduled to come out and interfere in our title match along with Undertaker, and what he did would have a lot to do with the finish.

But I was looking at Vince and thinking, "Me? What do you mean, me? That's why you have writers and all these other people around!"

Austin and I went out there after Hell in a Cell and didn't know what was going to happen at the end of our match. What would we do without the Mankind run-in? But Mick still came out.

He really is the toughest man alive.

Mick ran out and attacked Austin with the chair, but Steve took care of him immediately. Taker came out, hit Austin with a chair, threw me out of the ring, and then did the same to Mick. I got back up and blasted Taker with a chair, and then tried to attack Austin with it. Austin jumped off the top turnbuckle, taking me down, and then started hitting me with the chair.

As I lay on the mat with Austin standing over me, chair in hand, the referee called for the bell. Austin was bleeding. I—or someone—had drawn first blood. The match was over.

I was announced as the winner and new WWE Champion.

Monday Night Raw in Cleveland

Raw was in Cleveland the following night, so—after the match—Paul and I drove the two-plus hours to get there. When we arrived, I booked a double room, but not for Paul. He got his own room.

One bed was for me, and the other was for my WWE Championship.

The title slept by itself that night.

The thing is, I knew I was going to lose the title the following night. But in that moment, I didn't care. It was amazing. I went backstage after the match for a photo shoot with the title, as new champs customarily do. I could have pinched myself. No matter what happened from that point forward, I had accomplished something no one was ever going to be able to take away from me.

How many people have worn the WWE Title? At the time of this writing, there have been only fifty-one World Champions in the fifty-six-year history of the Title. They represent the best of the best in our industry. Now I had joined their ranks.

Even though I was able to keep it for just a day, it was a big deal. I barely slept.

The next day, Paul and I were getting ready to go to the show and he asked, "How did you sleep?" I told him I didn't sleep well. "I'm tired," I admitted. Paul jokingly replied, "Well you know, son, it's hard carrying the entire company on your back."

Paul had been around a lot longer than I had. He knew what holding the World Title meant within the business and, more important, to the person holding it.

"There's no way that anyone can understand what this momentous occasion means to my son and myself this evening," Paul Bearer said in the middle of the ring at the beginning of *Raw* the following night.

He was in character, but he wasn't lying!

Paul and I stood in the ring with Vince McMahon, Sgt. Slaughter, Jerry Brisco, and the WWE Championship, which was on display in a glass case before us. In a long promo, Paul said that I had always dreamed of being WWE Champion and that I had had posters of Undertaker all over my walls during twenty years as a child (not sure how that math works, but it worked with the crowd that night!). "Undertaker, tonight for the first time, you are standing in the shadow of your little brother!" Paul declared.

119

We were setting it up to look like I would challenge Taker again, only this time as WWE Champion.

That was when the glass broke and Austin walked out.

Austin got in Vince's face and said that, in a First Blood Match, "the winner is the one who draws first blood on his opponent." Looking at Vince and me, Steve explained as only Stone Cold Steve Austin could that it was Undertaker, not Kane, who had busted Austin open.

"The reason I'm out here is I want a rematch with Kane right here tonight!" Austin said. The crowd was on their feet. As Vince hemmed and hawed about a rematch, Austin interrupted him and said to the fans, "If you want a rematch give me a 'Hell yeah!'"

"*HELL YEAH!*" the crowd exploded.

After Austin bullied Vince and then Paul, and basically did everything he could to goad me into giving him a rematch, he said, "What I'm asking you for *the last time* is—Will you give me that rematch tonight?"

With the camera zoomed in on my face, I nodded my head up and down.

It was on.

As we talked backstage about how the match would go down that night, Austin said, "Kane goes out last, he's champion." He insisted on it. I thought that was pretty cool. Steve didn't have to do that.

We went back and forth throughout the match, inside and outside the ring. Paul hit Steve with his shoe. Taker came out. We tried to raise doubts in fans' minds as to whether Austin was going to win.

But all they wanted to see was Austin win the title back. They wanted it *so bad*!

When I set Steve up for a Tombstone piledriver, it looked like it might be all over for Austin. Yet he got out, kicked me in the stomach, and tried to give me the Stunner, his famous three-quarter facelock jawbreaker maneuver. I broke out of it and slung him into the ropes. When he came back, I tried to kick him and he ducked. He then kicked me and hit me with the Stunner. He went down and hooked my leg for the count.

The crowd was going *insane*! In unison the entire arena yelled, "1-2-3!"

Your new champion, Stone Cold Steve Austin!

Rocket Mortgage Fieldhouse that night was the most electric crowd I've ever been in front of. When I think about or am asked about the biggest moments in my career, the turning points, the Attitude Era, and anything else associated with Kane, I always go back to that night in Cleveland.

If Austin had just beaten me at the pay-per-view and at *Raw*, just blown through me, it wouldn't have meant anything. But for me to win the title at *King of the Ring* and lose it twenty-four hours later to arguably the biggest star in the history of our sport at the height of his career—that meant everything.

There are two schools of thinking when it comes to champions. Some bookers look at babyfaces or good guys and their ability to draw. Other bookers look at heels, but it's still all about the babyface and his ability to draw by playing off the heel.

Kane was an unbeatable monster. I gave Austin a goal he

wouldn't have had otherwise. The title switch shot him up even higher in popularity. That episode was one of the highest rated in *Raw* history at that point.

I was even more proud of losing the title to Steve than I had been of taking it from him because I thought I had really helped boost the momentum of the company. More than just helping Steve, I thought Kane was contributing in the biggest way yet to the success of WWE. That meant more to me than anything.

In addition to my public service, the Kane character has been the proudest achievement in my professional life, the reason I became known around the world—and frankly, it had a lot to do with getting me elected mayor.

Let's face it, Kane is the reason you're reading this book.

That magical night in the summer of 1998 might have boosted Austin, but I think it also cemented my legacy.

No matter what came next.

CHAPTER 5

WWE vs. THE VOLCANO

And Other Road Stories

Anyone who has worked for WWE will tell you that the hardest part of the job is the travel schedule. As a WWE Superstar, you can expect to spend upward of 250 nights a year on the road.

That schedule is year-round. There are no breaks for holidays or weekends. Sadly, you'll miss time with your family. You'll miss your kids' ball games, plays, parties, and dances.

That's the bad part. It's the trade-off for being a success in sports entertainment.

But in those many hours away from home, you'll also forge unbreakable bonds with some of your colleagues. You'll see the world and different cultures. And you'll have stories that most people won't believe.

Here are some of mine.

Sorry, Wrong Room

The bell had just rung, indicating the start of the last match at the TV taping in Anaheim. I was flying out of LAX the following morning and wanted to beat the crowd out of the arena. My match was close to the end of the night, so as soon as it was over, I hustled backstage and quickly got out of my ring gear. Instead of showering, I put on my workout clothes— shorts, a tank top, and sneakers—and ran out to the car.

I arrived at my hotel about forty-five minutes later. My appearance drew some stares as I waited in the check-in line. After all, I was six feet, eight inches tall, 315 pounds, with my hair in a ponytail that went halfway down my back. At the time, I was under the mask and I wore black paint around my eyes to blend in with the mask and make my appearance more ominous. As I sweated, the paint often rubbed off, leaving residue around my eyes that looked like runny mascara. All I wanted to do was get up to my room, go to bed, and grab a few hours of sleep.

Once I had my room key, I took the elevator up to the guest rooms. Luckily, the hall was empty, so no more weird looks. I got to my room, inserted the key in the lock, opened the door, and kind of tossed my bags into the room.

This was a habit I developed because the automatic door closers in hotels seemed to have it out for me. Inevitably, during the times when I pulled my bag behind me into the room, the door would shut right when I was halfway through and catch my bags, forcing me to struggle just to get into the room. So I had learned to push the bags through first.

So, in go the bags and I am walking through the door when I am greeted by shrieks of terror.

The room was already occupied by an elderly Japanese couple. If someone who looked like I did—immense, scant clothing, long hair, and mascara—burst into my hotel room unannounced, I would scream, too!

There was an awkward second or so, me just standing there, them standing on the bed, clutching each other in a desperate embrace and screaming in Japanese at the tops of their lungs.

I figured damage control was out of the question! I just grabbed my bags, mumbled an apology, and went back down to the lobby.

When I got there, I could see that the clerk was in a panic. It was clear that he was speaking with the folks who I had just scared the dickens out of.

"No, no, there's no need to call the police," he stammered. "Yes, we'll take care of your breakfast in the morning."

I got another room, which was, fortunately, unoccupied and had an uneventful rest of the night.

Of course, I've never again seen that elderly Japanese couple, but if I do, I hope they'll at least thank me for a complimentary breakfast!

Terre Haute, Illinois

The parking lot outside the Bank of Springfield Center in Springfield, Illinois, was small and always crowded. Fans stood on the adjacent sidewalk not thirty feet from the back-stage door. I was sitting in the driver's seat, waiting on my traveling partner, trainer Larry Heck, and punching into his GPS the coordinates for Terre Haute. Our next date was in Terre Haute, Indiana, the next state over. Larry slammed the trunk and jumped into the passenger's seat.

"Let's go," he said; I hit the Go button on his GPS, and away we went.

It was a nasty night. Lightning flashed across the sky, fol-lowed by the deep rumble of thunder. We drove through some side streets, got a burger at a fast-food drive-thru, and finally got onto the highway. Even with the bad weather, I was look-ing forward to an easy two-and-a-half-hour drive and an early night, hitting the sack a little after midnight.

The rain got worse, which slowed us somewhat. Larry and I filled the time with small talk and jokes. After a couple of hours, Larry pulled out his phone and started fiddling with it. I was lost in my own thoughts when I heard Larry mutter, "Oh, no."

Larry is a news junkie, so I figured he had seen something on a news website or social media.

"What's up?" I asked.

Larry giggled and replied, "Did you know there is a Terre Haute, *Illinois*?"

"Nope," I answered.

Larry laughed outright before exclaiming, "Well, you do now, because we're almost there."

"*What?!*" I exclaimed.

Larry showed me his phone screen. He'd pulled up the

mapping app and it showed us just a few miles from Terre Haute, Illinois.

"Oh, man," I said; Larry hit a couple of buttons on his GPS and, sure enough, it showed we were in Terre Haute, *Illinois*, and not Terre Haute, *Indiana*.

In my haste to leave the arena, I'd selected the first Terre Haute the GPS displayed. How many Terre Hautes are there?

"Wonderful, just wonderful," I thought to myself.

Larry punched in the correct destination, then we turned around and drove back through the thunderstorms, passing through Springfield, where we could see the arena from the highway, before finally pulling into our hotel in the right Terre Haute at 5 a.m.

Larry and I had a combined thirty-five years on the road. Knowing how embarrassing this episode would be, we made a pact to never tell anyone.

Of course, the next day, I couldn't resist. As soon as I walked into the locker room, I announced, "Y'all will never guess what Larry and I did last night!"

The Reggie Jackson Incident

American Airlines was on strike and it had thrown a monkey wrench into my travel plans. I was supposed to fly from LaGuardia Airport in New York to Miami, but my flight was cancelled due to the strike. Since Miami was one of American's hubs, most commercial flights going there were on American, and they were all grounded.

After two days trying to get out, I was booked on the last seat on a Delta flight. Beggars can't be choosers, so I was happy to get any seat at all, even the middle seat that I had.

Not that I was looking forward to flying for three hours in such cramped quarters. But it beat the alternative of missing my booking in Miami.

All of these thoughts were running through my mind as I stood in line at the ticket counter at LaGuardia. I was, admittedly, not in the best of moods when the guy behind me said, "Man, you're a big guy. Are you a wrestler or something?"

The question rubbed me the wrong way. I was frustrated and didn't want to talk to anyone. Without turning around, I responded sarcastically, "Yes, I'm a wrestler, not a something."

I immediately regretted saying that. I was trying to be funny sarcastic, but it came out as plain old mean sarcastic.

The guy didn't respond, and I felt about six inches tall. Just because I was having a bad day didn't mean that I should have been taking it out on anyone else.

Still facing forward, I said, "I'm sorry. I was trying to be funny. I've had a bad couple of days."

"That's okay. I hear you. People say stuff like that to me all the time. I'm Reggie Jackson," he replied.

That statement hung in the air for a second as I digested it. Yes, the voice sounded familiar. Now, I'd have to play it cool. For the first time, I snuck a look at the figure behind me. Sure enough, it was "Mr. October" Reggie Jackson himself!

I was mortified and embarrassed. Karma had come back around quickly. It was my turn to go to the ticket counter so

I mumbled another apology and left with my proverbial tail between my legs.

For many years, I took for granted how much my WWE fame touched people. Despite pursuing careers that put me in the spotlight, I'm a natural introvert and I've had to make an effort to come out of my shell. Early in my career, I was not as friendly and outgoing as I should have been. Not because I was mean and arrogant, but because I was shy and uncomfortable.

Then, one day, Crystal and I were having lunch at a restaurant in Knoxville. I had just returned home from a road trip and was tired and grumpy. I was starting to get frustrated as people stopped at our table and asked for a picture or an autograph.

"Man, I wished they'd leave me alone," I muttered.

Crystal replied, "Honey, what you need to understand is...because you're on TV, meeting you is one of the most exciting things that some people will ever experience."

I wouldn't admit it at the time, but she was right. It wasn't about me, it was about giving people a good experience. The choice was up to me. I could look at this attention, people wanting autographs and pictures, as a burden and a hassle. Or I could think about it as an opportunity to bring folks joy and happiness.

I decided to choose the latter. I could put a smile on my face and be polite and friendly for a few minutes if it meant making other folks happy.

Then, a funny thing happened. I began to like it. In fact, I felt rewarded and fulfilled. I learned a couple of life's lessons.

One is that everything is a matter of perspective, and you get to choose what perspective to take. If you want to be miserable, you can be, no matter how good your circumstances.

If you choose to be happy, you will find happiness, even when life might not be going as you'd like it to go.

The second lesson is that living is about giving. You get what you give. If you are a jerk to people, guess what? You'll be treated like a jerk. If you are nice to folks, on the other hand, they are likely to be good to you.

There is no feeling of satisfaction like the one I feel when someone asks to shake my hand and thanks me for giving them years of entertainment. I mean, after all, if they hadn't watched, I wouldn't have had a job!

I've had people tell me that, as teenagers, they were depressed and felt like outcasts. They also told me that the Kane character, himself an outcast, had inspired them and helped them through a tough time.

I once had a waiter in a restaurant tell me that his grandma had been diagnosed with a terminal illness a few years before. She loved WWE and I was one of her favorites. She lived another eighteen months during which the two of them watched WWE together every chance they could.

He thanked *me* for that!

Those experiences are a blessing and they are something most people will never experience. When people ask me what's the best thing about being Kane, I tell them that it's the ability to bring joy and happiness into people's lives.

It's one of the greatest gifts God has ever given me.

I look back on that day in LaGuardia Airport, and some other instances, and think about what I should have done differently.

Mr. Jackson, if you're reading this, my apologies. I've grown a lot since then.

And I'd love an autograph, if you are so inclined!

The Volcano

On April 14, 2010, the volcano at Eyjafjallajökull, Iceland, erupted, spewing ash into the atmosphere and creating an ash cloud that led to the grounding of commercial jetliners across Europe.

Which just happened to be where WWE was touring at the time.

Millions of people across Europe had their travel plans disrupted. For me, it was the most arduous few days of travel that I've ever experienced.

I hadn't been following the news so I didn't know anything about the eruption until I arrived in the lobby of our hotel in Hamburg, Germany, on my way to a workout at the local gym. I stopped to talk with our market rep about the travel plans for that day. We had planned to take a charter flight to Zurich that night after the show in Hamburg.

"Haven't you seen the news about the volcano?" he asked. "Air travel is shut down. It looks like we are going to stay here tonight and then take a train to Zurich."

Alrighty then! I still didn't think much about it. WWE arranges all our travel when we tour in foreign countries, so it wasn't like I could do anything about it anyway. My main concern was just getting to the bus on time. After that, I followed the rest of the herd.

When I got to the gym and saw that every television station was following the volcanic eruption story, I realized it was a big deal. By the time I got back to the hotel, WWE officials, road agents Ricky Steamboat and Fit Finlay, along with the local event staff were making sure that everyone was aware of the change in travel plans for that night. Plans for the rest of the tour, they said, were uncertain. At the same time, another WWE team was touring in the United Kingdom, where things were even worse. That crew was expected to be stranded in Belfast until conditions improved, whenever that might be.

Early the next day, we left the hotel to catch the first train to Zurich. We took just our gear bags. The rest of our luggage went into a cargo van, which was to meet us in Zurich. I had a ticket in the first-class cabin on the train. Unlike in an airplane, first class and coach in the train were the same, except first-class ticketholders had their own little room to sit in.

It's a little over five hundred miles from Hamburg to Zurich, which meant about an eight-hour train ride. When the train first took off, I thought we'd be there in no time. We were flying at more than one hundred miles per hour. But I soon realized that would not be the case. The problem was we were stopping at a station every few minutes. We'd be at the station for a minute or two and take off again.

There was a snack bar on one of the other cars and, after a few hours on the train, boredom and hunger drove me to step out of my cabin and head that way.

What I saw shocked me.

At all those stops we were making, it seemed that no one got off the train. But *a lot* of people had gotten on.

The car was so packed with people that I couldn't get to the snack bar. At the far end of the cabin, baggage was stacked from floor to ceiling! I turned around, went back into my cabin, and grumpily settled in for the rest of the trip.

We arrived in Zurich to board tour buses, which took us to the building just in time so we could do the show.

After the event, we waited to hear the plans for the rest of the tour. Originally, we had been scheduled for another day in Europe and then a final show in Istanbul, Turkey. Everyone was excited about the Istanbul show. It was our debut there and it was sold out, with an expected crowd of twenty thousand.

Back in Stamford, WWE personnel were scrambling to figure out what to do. Airline travel was disrupted and spotty. Meanwhile, ground travel was quickly booked. Later, I read in *Time* magazine that John Cleese of Monty Python fame racked up a $5,400 taxicab bill trying to get home to London from Norway. WWE had to deal with the same thing as all forms of alternative transportation—trains, ferries, and buses—were quickly becoming unavailable.

Over the following couple of hours, we got sporadic information. The first bit of bad news was that the show in Istanbul had been cancelled. WWE was trying to get us back to the United States as soon as possible to make sure we were there in time for TV.

Finally, we were told our tour buses would take us to the

airport in Geneva. Since our drivers would legally be "timed out" when they got there, meaning they would have to take eight hours off to rest, we transferred into two luxury coaches that were going to take us from Geneva to Madrid, Spain, about nine hundred miles, then fly on a charter to Newark, New Jersey.

It sounded tedious, but at least there was a plan.

The four-hour drive to Geneva went smoothly. When we arrived at the airport, we saw two nice tour buses that we thought were waiting for us.

But our driver sped past them. A little farther on, we saw two small, cargo-type vans—think hotel shuttle buses. Those were the vehicles that were taking us across France and deep into Spain.

These misnamed "luxury coaches" were so small that we had to leave some of our personnel at the airport in Geneva because there was no room for them on the buses. As I walked around the bus to which I had been assigned, I noticed the tires were bald and missing a lug nut here and there. Scott Aycock from our security team used to drive a tour bus. We made eye contact after both of us saw the condition of the tires.

Scott just shook his head.

Still, we piled onto the buses, humans and luggage, and took off. Our bus had a bathroom. Unfortunately, the driver didn't have the key, and it was locked. Now, keep in mind, we were already working on a twenty-hour day. I was lucky to have a seat to myself and fell asleep with my head against the window. When I woke up, we made a quick stop to go to the bathroom and grab some drinks and snacks.

By this time, the sun was rising. Traffic was blowing by us. I looked at the speedometer and saw we were going only about forty miles an hour on the highway. We had planned on arriving in Madrid a few hours before the flight left. WWE had even reserved day rooms at the airport hotel so that we could shower and relax while we waited.

"I bet they thought we were going to be going more than forty miles an hour," I thought to myself dejectedly.

But there was an even bigger problem. The airport in Madrid had a midnight curfew. Our plane was scheduled to be back in the United States the next morning.

In other words, it was leaving at midnight—with or without us.

Additionally, our drivers spoke French. None of us did. So we faced a communication barrier. Luckily, Rey Mysterio said something in Spanish and one of the drivers perked up and told Rey he, too, spoke Spanish.

At that moment, Rey became the most important person on our bus!

We stopped in Barcelona for a late lunch. At this point, we were thirty hours from Hamburg. Madrid was another four hundred miles. As slow as our bus was going, we'd be lucky to get there by the following week, much less before midnight.

After a quick bite, it was back on the bus. No one was happy. The trip had been grueling, and you could see it on everyone's face. By this time, our poor bus was feeling its load. The engine strained to keep up with traffic on the highway. It was slightly unnerving to see the drivers pull out the owner's manual, point to it, and speak to each other in hushed voices.

At one point, we pulled over at a convenience store and one of the drivers ran inside, returned with some engine oil, popped the hood, and poured it in.

On and on we drove. Hours turned into days, or at least it seemed like it. By now, dusk was settling over the Iberian Peninsula. We finally began seeing road signs for Madrid. Our hopes rose just like the mountains in front of us.

Although I was born in Madrid, I was unaware of its geography. Little did I know that it lies about twenty miles south of the Sierra de Guadarrama mountain range—through which we were now driving.

Mountain ranges and an overloaded "luxury coach" are not a good combination. A turtle could have beaten our little bus up the steep hills. Every vehicle on the road, even the semitrucks, was flying past us. We would get to the top of one peak, build up some pretty good speed going downhill, and then be confronted with an even steeper climb when we started up the next hill.

Maybe it was my imagination, but I think one of the drivers even made the sign of the cross as the little-bus-that-could started up a particularly steep grade!

What was not my imagination were the warning lights on the dashboard. They were lit up like a Christmas tree. I thought that, at any second, we'd hear *Bang! Pop!*—signals that our bus's engine had finally blown—and our trip would end on the side of the road.

Miraculously, that didn't happen. We cleared the last peak and saw the lights of Madrid before us. We were going to make it after all.

The bus seemed to share our newfound enthusiasm. It picked up speed as we entered the outskirts of Madrid and, finally, the airport. It was eleven o'clock or so. The midnight curfew was dangling over our heads like the Sword of Damocles.

It was going to be close, but we felt we were going to make it.

We pulled up to the main terminal . . . only to discover our flight wasn't leaving from there. The international terminal was on the other side of the airport. The bus was not equipped with GPS, however, so we weren't sure where to go.

Until this point, everyone had remained in fairly good spirits, talking with one another. Now, you could hear a pin drop.

"You've got to be kidding me," I thought to myself, as I'm sure everyone else did. "We've been traveling for like two days and we're going to miss the flight because we got lost in the terminal!?!"

Luckily, Fit Finlay's bus was already at the correct terminal and he guided us in via cell phone. We unloaded our bags, sprinted through security, boarded the plane and lifted off at 11:53 p.m., a full seven minutes before the airport closed, which would have stranded us in Spain for who knew how long.

By the time we arrived in Newark, forty-six hours had elapsed since our departure from Hamburg.

As almost always happens in WWE, the show went on. We arrived in Newark around midnight on Saturday. We had Sunday off.

On Monday, *Raw* was broadcast live from Newark's Izod Arena, as if nothing had even happened.

CHAPTER 6

BROTHERS OF DESTRUCTION

After my showdown with Austin, I began tag-teaming with Mankind. It wasn't our first time as a team, but the program Mick and I would work against Austin and Taker, rivals who had briefly teamed up, would have a lot do with the next big evolution for the Kane character.

Kane and Mankind: Have a Nice Day!

On a *Monday Night Raw* in July 1998, just two weeks after I had dropped the WWE Title to Austin, Mick and I defeated The New Age Outlaws, "Road Dogg" Jesse James and "Badd Ass" Billy Gunn, for the WWE Tag Team Titles. We would then lose the titles to Austin and Taker. Mick and I would then regain the tag titles from Austin and Taker in a Fatal 4-Way Match on *Raw* that included the New Age

Outlaws and The Nation of Domination's The Rock and D'Lo Brown.

There was a lot of switching back and forth during that time for everyone at the top of the card, in both titles and partners. All of it had to do with pushing WWE's franchise player, Austin, particularly building up his big match at *Summer-Slam* with Undertaker.

Mick and I had a lot of fun working together because we were such good friends. One story I'll never forget took place in a Hell in the Cell Match on *Raw* when Kane had a falling out with Mankind.

Mick was adamant about using thumbtacks in our match. He thought it would add a lot to Kane vs. Mankind. I didn't want to use thumbtacks. I was like, "Mick, we're already using chairs and doing all this other cool stuff. We don't need the thumbtacks!"

Because I had the utmost respect for him, we ended up using thumbtacks.

The deal was, I would not have to fall in the tacks. Mankind wanted to use them, and it was Mick and Mick alone who was going to suffer any consequences. Fine by me.

When we got to that spot in the match, Mick wound me up for a piledriver and when my back went toward his face, I lost my balance.

I not only fell right into the thumbtacks—I sat right down in them.

So, not only were thumbtacks sticking all over me including my hands—which *really* hurts, like paper cuts, but much worse—my backside was covered in tacks! Almost my entire butt was silver. Not very monstrous, to say the least. It was really embarrassing.

I had so many tacks in the soles of my boots that I was picking them out for two months. *"I told you we didn't need thumbtacks!"* I yelled at Mick. He just laughed.

Mick and I were great together, particularly as two dark characters. I remember one night when Shawn Michaels was on commentary and he said that what made us so dangerous is that you have one guy, Kane, who doesn't feel anything, and another, Mankind, who "likes it" (the pain).

Wrestling is the weirdest business in the world. A business where, after a guy hits you in the back with a steel chair, you thank him later for it; and when your friend helps drive you into hundreds of thumbtacks, you both end up agreeing it was a good match!

At *SummerSlam* that year, Mick and I were supposed to defend our tag team titles in a hardcore tag team match against Road Dogg and Billy Gunn. I no-showed and therefore Mankind had to wrestle alone. Needless to say, the New Age Outlaws won that de facto Handicap Match and became the new tag team champions.

After being announced as new champs, Road Dogg and Billy told Mankind they were going to put him in the garbage "where you belong!" They tossed Mick in a dumpster, closed the lid, and walked off.

Once they were gone, I popped up out of the dumpster holding a sledgehammer, ready to smash Mick's head in. And

I did. No one could see Mankind lying in the bottom of the dumpster, but they could hear it when I caved his skull in with the hammer.

What they actually heard was me smashing a giant watermelon. Kane was Gallagher for a night!

But perhaps the funniest part about that match had nothing to do with what took place in the ring. *SummerSlam* was at Madison Square Garden that year and I remember pushing a dumpster backstage. Being New York City, of course, everything was run by the unions.

As I was pushing it along, a bunch of workers said that I couldn't touch the dumpster. They said it was against union rules.

I was like, "Okay . . ."

I told them that, rules or not, I had to push the dumpster from backstage to the main stage for the match I was about to have. The union guys said that would be all right, because once it got to the stage it would no longer be under their jurisdiction. Then it would become a "prop."

That night I learned the technical definitions of a "dumpster" and a "prop." Pretty silly, right? There were actually regulations that forbade me from pushing around a dumpster for a wrestling match? Ridiculous. I wasn't as overtly political then as I would become later, but maybe that was the real beginning of me becoming a libertarian!

Mankind and Kane were a pretty good team, while it lasted. But it was certainly not the most famous tag team I was part of.

Not even close.

1998: A Year of Brotherly Destruction

As we slowly built toward the Brothers of Destruction throughout 1998, I didn't know that was what we were doing. Neither did Taker. I don't think many, if anyone, in WWE realized that was where we were heading.

Sometimes, people think WWE has everything mapped out. That's not always the case, and it certainly wasn't in the evolution of the relationship between Kane and Undertaker.

After Austin beat me for the title at the *Raw* in Cleveland after *King of the Ring*, Undertaker stepped over the ropes to stare down Stone Cold Steve Austin, The Rattlesnake. When Taker turned to leave the ring, Austin caught him with a Stunner, and fans saw both Taker and Kane lying flat on their backs.

As Austin was walking up the ramp celebrating with the entire Rocket Mortgage Fieldhouse going insane, Taker and I both sat up, Deadman style. Then we both stood up simultaneously.

We stared down Austin, who by now was standing at the top of the ramp. He looked right back at us, his eyes locked on us two brothers.

That was how *Raw* went off the air that night.

Imagine the scene. Many of you might remember it. The biggest star in the wrestling world just winning the WWE Title facing off against two of the company's most popular characters at the height of the Attitude Era.

It's a time I'll never forget, and I know many fans feel the same way.

Little by little, the Brothers of Destruction act was taking shape. We dropped seeds at different intervals for months. The running theme that gave birth to this formidable alliance would be the same at virtually every turn: The enemy of my enemy is my friend.

The first seed Taker and I planted, as I discussed earlier, was at the *Raw* before the 1998 *Royal Rumble* in State College, Pennsylvania, when I ran out to save Mark from DX. Everyone thought I was there to save my brother, and I was—until I burned him alive in a casket!

By the summer of 1998, we were starting to pair together more often.

I would play a significant part in the Austin vs. Undertaker main event at *SummerSlam*. Remember, I had abandoned Mankind in the tag match earlier in the night, before smashing Mick with a sledgehammer. I'd like to think that was revenge for the thumbtacks!

During the Austin–Taker main event, I walked down and stood at ringside midmatch. Taker ordered me to the back. I followed his orders.

Austin ended up defeating Taker, and when Mark stepped out of the ring, I joined him once again. Undertaker and Kane stood at the entrance staring down the victorious Stone Cold.

Steve celebrated his win, but his eyes were fixed on Mark and me. His reaction to us was important to our story line development. Stone Cold saw Undertaker and Kane standing there and seemed be thinking, without saying a word, "Oh, no."

To have Steve acknowledge us in that way really helped

sell our alliance, because everybody realized Austin was genuinely worried about us. The rowdy, beer-swillin' everyman-hero who doesn't worry about anything was all of a sudden really concerned about Deadman and the Big Red Machine and what they might do to him.

Sometimes subtleties like this are the most important aspects of our business. WWE is often accused of being over the top because, well, we are, but it is the little things like Steve's reaction that night that end up being the best material. People often miss that.

Similarly, I did very little in Steve and Taker's *Summer-Slam* match. Merely walking out intermittently was all it took to reveal, for the first time explicitly, that Undertaker and Kane were working together.

Believe it or not, even at this point I still wasn't privy to where all this was headed, and I don't think Taker was, either. Sometimes, the most memorable things that happen in WWE are not preplanned, but instead evolve organically.

The evolution of the Brothers of Destruction is a perfect example.

Though the Kane character was originally created for the sole purpose of giving Undertaker a monster heel opponent, Vince knew that, over time, WWE could make more money if the brothers joined forces rather than opposing each other. The fans had been dying to see us together, going all the way back to that night at *Raw* in State College, Pennsylvania, in 1998.

I was completely happy to be working with Mick after losing the title to Austin, and if after that I had been featured in the lower card and then phased out altogether, I wouldn't have been surprised. I would have been happy for my success. Few in our business get to that level—for any period of time.

Performance and timing are both important, but even those components aren't necessarily everything. Isaac Yankem had been a failure, partly because I didn't do it very well. I thought I did a good job as fake Diesel, but in the end, I *was* fake Diesel, a character whose shelf life proved to be short.

After playing two characters that had gone nowhere, I was now Kane, in the mix with Austin, Taker, Mick, and The Rock, for however long this character would last. After *WrestleMania*, so many thought I would just fade away. I was constantly appreciating the fact that I hadn't.

It was all just sort of happening, and when I was working with Mick, I had no idea that six months later I would be allied with Undertaker as half of one of the greatest tag teams in WWE history.

At the next pay-per-view, *Breakdown*, held on September 27, 1998, the main event was a triple threat match among Kane, Undertaker, and Austin for the title, with the stipulation that Mark and I could not pin each other. It was, by design, a de facto Handicap Match.

But we both Chokeslammed Austin. More importantly, we *both pinned* Steve.

Stone Cold had lost the world title. But who won it?

That night, no one knew—Vince grabbed the title, ran through the backstage area, and jumped into a limousine. Austin chased him.

As the show went off the air, Vince stood by his limo and

held the title high, yelling at Steve, "You see this? You don't have it anymore! It's mine! *It's mine!*"

Then Vince flipped Austin the bird, as Stone Cold so often did to him, and sped off.

It was awesome.

As for the actual match that night, I remember Austin, Taker, and me sitting in the locker room feeling disappointed because it didn't appear to have gotten the reaction we wanted. We knew what the audience really wanted was for Austin to beat either Taker or me, and when that didn't happen, for us it just didn't seem to gel. We were bummed.

But Vince thought it was great. He was good with everything we did. In WWE, sometimes the performers are hard on themselves because they think they didn't deliver or underperformed in some fashion, while Vince is happy as long as he got what he wanted out of it.

Vince wanted Austin to lose the title and for us to do the double pin that night. That was what happened, so the boss was happy. Steve lost but still looked strong—what human being could possibly pop out of being pinned by both Kane and Undertaker?!

If you look at the entirety of the angle, to this day, so many fans remember Vince standing beside his limo at the end of the show, holding up the title and shooting Austin the bird. Vince's facial expression alone was priceless—again, the subtleties!

We were a part of that, and even though we were unhappy with our particular performances in the ring, Vince saw the bigger picture. He always does.

While much of what happens in WWE is more spontaneous than many realize, it's also no secret that Vince has the ability to look into the future and see story lines and just about everything else—Bruce Prichard says Vince was talking about a concept similar to the WWE Network as far back as the mid-1980s during the Hulkamania era!—probably better than anyone else in the history of sports entertainment.

Case in point: That same night, as Austin, Taker, and I were sitting backstage, Vince said to me, "Don't go stone-faced under your mask because, at some point, you're not going to be wearing it anymore."

Steve snickered. He asked Vince, "Why do you want to take his mask off? He's doing great!" I was thinking the same thing.

But, as we all know, my mask eventually did come off, a move that breathed even more life into the ever-evolving Kane character.

But the point is, Vince always thinks long-term. My mask wouldn't come off for another five years, but on that night way back in 1998, Vince was already envisioning it.

The next night, the Brothers of Destruction would take another step.

The Brothers Destroy Vince McMahon

"I'm about to present the WWE Championship," Vince said in the middle of the ring on *Raw* in Detroit, Michigan. The vacant title that both Taker and I had won the previous night—but one that neither of us had really won, since we both pinned Austin—lay unclaimed in a glass case.

"However, if you recall, the deal was, Undertaker and Kane, you would get the title shot as long as you kept Stone Cold Steve Austin away from me," Vince scolded. "But three times, three times in less than a week, Austin has brutally attacked me!" The crowd cheered for that.

"So, let me say this, you didn't live up to your end of the deal—*I'm not gonna live up to mine*!" Vince growled right in Taker's face.

Vince then said that, at the next pay-per-view, Taker and I would have to battle it out for the title, with Austin as the guest referee. "Whether you like it or not!" he added.

We didn't like it. So we broke Vince's leg with the steel stairs.

"*Oh my God! Oh my God!*" Jim Ross screamed. I was pretty much screaming the same thing on the inside! When you are supposed to break the boss's leg in a story line, you *really don't want* to break the boss's leg! I was so nervous about that angle that night.

Years after this, when I would end up Tombstoning Linda McMahon on the stage, her safety was the most important thing on my mind. Believe me, there was *no way* she was going to get hurt.

I had the same supercautious attitude with Vince that night. How could I not?!

But while I was nervous, Taker was ready to *hammer* him! Vince always took great pleasure in ribbing Mark, so Mark was going to take any opportunity he could find to get him back. Taker wasn't going to hurt him in reality, but if he had an opportunity to Chokeslam Vince, he was going to *Chokeslam* him! If he was going to Tombstone Vince, he was going to *piledrive* him!

And that night, if Mark was supposed to break Vince's leg with the steel stairs, he was definitely going to have some fun with it.

Vince would later start ribbing me in the same way he always had with Taker. I would be out in the ring with someone that didn't make sense on any level or in some angle I thought was completely ridiculous, and Vince would say, "You're never going to stop paying your dues, Glenn!" and then walk off laughing.

Though that night I was nervous that we might hurt Vince, six years later I would end up having the same attitude as Taker!

Vince is one of the greatest performers in the history of our business, and part of that means that he's not afraid to get beat up, look foolish, take risks, or do any of the many things he has always done to make the Mr. McMahon character such a great heel.

And he would never have complained or held it against you if you actually hurt him. That risk is always part of the deal in our business, and he understood that.

As 1999 approached, Undertaker and Kane began drifting apart. At the *Rock Bottom* pay-per-view in Vancouver, Canada, in December 1998, I interfered in the Buried Alive Match between Austin and Taker, where I Tombstoned Mark and then pushed him into an open grave. Steve then buried him with a backhoe for the win. So much for brotherly love!

That same month, December's WWE *Raw* magazine featured both Mark and me on the cover holding sledgehammers, with the caption "Bang Your Head!!! A look at Taker and Kane's Greatest Hitz!!!"

We certainly had many hits in 1998, a year that proved pivotal for the Attitude Era. But for Taker and me it will always go down as the year the Brothers of Destruction were born. Our alliance will always be the most famous pairing for either of us, and it was a go-to for the company for the following two decades.

Neither I nor Taker has ever taken for granted that enduring fan appreciation.

CHAPTER 7

KANE AND X-PAC

I could write an entire book about the Brothers of Destruction alone. Undertaker and I joining forces has had almost as long a shelf life as our individual characters. As I'm writing this chapter in the summer of 2019, it has been less than a year since we last tag-teamed together.

Even though I'm a mayor now and Taker no longer works a full-time schedule with WWF, as Taker mentioned in the foreword—you still really never know when we might pop up again!

One of the next steps in the evolution of Kane, predictably, involved Undertaker and led to one of the most memorable tag teams in my career: Kane and X-Pac, aka Sean Waltman.

After the Buried Alive Match between Taker and Austin, The Corporation, led by Mr. McMahon, had me committed to an insane asylum as punishment for helping Austin. I was then forced to join The Corporation in order to stay out of the asylum. It didn't take long for The Corporation to betray me and I was thrown out of the group. Fine by me!

The way that split went down pushed me into a tag team with X-Pac. I'll never forget the night we made our pairing official at the Rupp Arena in Lexington, Kentucky.

X-Pac and I were in a tag match against Big Show (aka Paul Wight) and "Hardcore" Bob Holly. While I was on the floor fighting with Show, Taker came out and Chokeslammed X-Pac in the middle of the ring. I didn't see it.

Taker came down and attacked both Big Show and Bob Holly with the steel stairs, helping me. After Taker and I beat up Show and Holly for a bit, I followed Taker up the entrance ramp to leave. It looked like Undertaker and Kane had reunited.

But then I turned around and returned to the ring to check on X-Pac, leaving Taker behind. A frustrated Undertaker grabbed me, saying, "It's over!" He wanted me to forget about X-Pac and leave with him.

That was when the replay of Undertaker Chokeslamming X-Pac, which I had missed, showed up on the TitanTron. Taker bowed his head. He didn't want me to see this. His facial expressions and body language showed that he knew he had been caught with his hand in the cookie jar.

Taker then turned around to face me, apologetically, but I wasn't having it. I Chokeslammed Taker. The crowd went ballistic.

"*Kane! Kane! Kane!*" Jim Ross yelled. "*Chokeslam! Chokeslam!* Who's your daddy, Undertaker?" he screamed.

Then I picked up X-Pac, slung his limp body across my shoulder, and walked back up the entrance ramp. At one point, X-Pac regained awareness of what was going on and I put him down. Still dazed, he looked around and realized that I had just chosen him over Undertaker—that Kane had just beaten up his own brother to ally with him.

X-Pac hugged me. The crowd went nuts again. It was a great feel-good moment.

"Kane has never had a heart until he met X-Pac!" screamed J.R.

This was the first time Kane had really turned babyface. I was still The Big Red Machine, but X-Pac was my little buddy, and I would stand up for him.

X-Pac would be instrumental in giving Kane more depth. Before our pairing, I had always been just a silent, brooding killer who destroyed everything. I remember X-Pac and I once teased a break-up in Kansas City, Missouri. X-Pac chased me down backstage, and found me crying, thanks to the Visine we had put in my eyes.

Kane was evolving.

Losing Owen

On a more somber note, I will never forget the day in 1999, during my run with Sean, that we lost Owen Hart, who fell from the top of Kansas City's Kemper Arena while making his entrance. X-Pac and I were wrestling D'Lo Brown and Mark Henry on that pay-per-view, but nobody really remembers what happened in their matches that night.

I remember when Owen came through the back on the gurney. You could tell he was no longer with us. I remember seeing Vince completely torn up, sitting with his head in his hands at Gorilla.

I called Crystal and told her what had happened and that I thought he was hurt really bad. She hadn't seen it happen. No viewers watching at home had, which we wouldn't learn until later. Crystal thought I meant he had fallen off the ring apron and I had to explain how dire the situation was.

Afterward, we were criticized for continuing the show, but I can tell you that—in that moment—no one knew what to do: not Vince, me, the wrestlers, the crew—no one. No one was barking orders or demanding this or that.

We were all in such a state of shock that we simply continued doing the only thing we knew, which was putting on a show. No one's head was in their match that night. It was just going through the motions because we didn't know what else to do. It wasn't taken in stride in the least, and anyone who suggests otherwise really doesn't know what in the hell they're talking about.

Owen, who was just thirty-four years old when he died, was loved and adored by everyone in that locker room. It was a heartbreaking loss for all of us.

Babyface Kane?

Thanks to X-Pac, Kane's character got a human element that it had never had before. For the first time, I was allowed to shine as a babyface. The matches were almost always structured the same way—X-Pac would get beat up most of the time, I would eventually step in and save him and make the big comeback. X-Pac would sell (in wrestling parlance, making an opponent's move look impactful) like crazy to our opponents and was always so unselfish in the ring.

Working with X-Pac, Kane now had feelings that went beyond his trademark staples: anger and misery. Sometimes, fans watching his shows even caught glimpses of comedy, something I would really delve into in a big way later in my career.

One of the most memorable—and hilarious—vignettes happened because of X-Pac: the first time Kane ever spoke without using the voice box.

"This has been a long time coming," X-Pac said on *Monday Night Raw*, right after we had regained the World Tag Team Titles. "If you ain't down with me and the Big Red Machine being the tag team champs again, Kane has got two words for ya."

Road Dogg handed me my voice box, and I put it up to my throat to speak. X-Pac snatched it out of my hand and said, "You don't need this damn thing anymore."

Then, as X-Pac held the mic up to my mask, I gargled in a low, scary tone, "*Suck it!*"

The crowd became unglued. It was powerful and comical at the same time. When we were talking about it backstage before the show, I had thought it sounded completely ridiculous.

It wasn't. It proved to be a powerful segment that many remember to this day.

X-Pac and I were close. He was one of my favorite tag team

partners. He would also stand up for me politically, always looking out for me backstage. If he didn't like some angle I was in or the way I was being treated, he wouldn't hesitate to go to Vince or Shane McMahon. He would say, "Glenn's awesome! What are y'all trying to do?"

X-Pac thought I was a tremendous talent and always wanted me to look good. He always had my back.

To this day, X-Pac and I still talk. We have been through a lot together. I'm not saying we hung out after the shows, because we ran with different crowds. There were also bad times when X-Pac was dealing with personal issues and he dropped off the radar for a while.

Still, we've kept in touch over the years, and he's in a great place now. I'm happy for all his continuing success. He deserves it.

But, as all tag teams eventually do, we split up.

We always wanted our blow off to be a big match. X-Pac had an idea: a steel cage death match with weapons hanging off the side, exploding bombs and any other crazy stuff we could come up with.

X-Pac wanted pyrotechnics. He had already shot me in the face with a flame-throwing bazooka. Triple H had done the same thing to me. It had become sort of a D-Generation X thing to try to burn up Kane.

Now that I think of it, all of that might have been out of a desire for revenge.

The worst flame-throwing incident that went down between Kane and DX had to be what I accidentally did to Chyna one night on *Raw*. X-Pac and Hunter ended up shooting me with fiery bazookas. But all I had was a double-barrel prop gun filled with flash paper. When I hit a button, it looked like flames were coming out of my hands.

I was in the ring and Chyna was holding Triple H's arms behind his back so I could inflict damage (Chyna and I were both part of The Corporation at the time).

I shot fire from my hand. The plan was for me to aim at Hunter, who would step aside so that the flame ball hit Chyna instead.

But when I pulled the trigger, the flash paper failed to expand as it flew through the air. Instead, it remained wadded up like a spitball. Usually, the flash paper was relatively harmless—"poof!" and the flame was gone instantly. But not this time. Nope, this time a flaming spitball shot across the ring with a vengeance.

I had been intending to hit Chyna's chest, but the flaming spitball hit her in the worst place possible...in her eye. Inside, I was thinking "Oh, my God!" but I still had to remain in character as Kane.

It was like the famous scene in the 1983 comedy *A Christmas Story*, where Ralphie's mom kept telling him to be cautious with his Red Ryder BB gun. "You'll shoot your eye out," she warned.

I kept thinking, "Don't hit her in the eye!" Then I hit her in the eye!

I felt so terrible. Thankfully, Chyna was okay. I think she was angry that it burned her eyelashes off more than anything.

But I had reason to be worried. Though flash paper is relatively harmless compared to some of the other pyrotechnic stunts we did, it is the routine moves and stunts we use—which we assume are safer—that typically result in the greatest number of injuries.

Most wrestlers will tell you the same thing.

As for X-Pac's idea of us breaking up the tag team in a steel cage death match with weapons and pyro—another wrestler, named Bill Goldberg, killed it. I don't mean that Bill lobbied Vince to stop it from happening. In fact, Bill never knew X-Pac had this idea. But Bill used the same technology in his own entrances.

X-Pac's idea was for the big massive sparklers, or "squibs," to erupt during the match. X-Pac thought we could even use them as weapons against one another. We thought it would have looked pretty awesome!

Then X-Pac explained his idea to Vince. Vince said, "Aren't squibs the things that Goldberg stands in?" He wanted to know why the fans would think those squibs would hurt us, when Bill was able to stand in them unscathed, snorting smoke. He thought we would look like two wimps compared to Goldberg.

Vince was right. The match never happened.

Wrestling at *WrestleMania 2000* with a Broken Hand

After X-Pac and I split, I formed a tag team with Rikishi. Going back to routine moves sometimes being the most dangerous, on the last *SmackDown* before *WrestleMania* in San Antonio, Texas, Rikishi and I took on The Dudley Boyz,

Bubba Ray Dudley and D-Von Dudley. I clotheslined D-Von coming off the top rope and, when I landed to roll up to my feet, my fingers got stuck in the mat. That bent my fingers straight back and broke my hand.

It was the most serious injury I'd had.

So, at *WrestleMania 2000* five days later, it was Kane and Rikishi vs. X-Pac and Road Dogg. I wrestled the entire match with a broken hand.

You never know when those kinds of accidents can happen. I've probably done that clothesline move more than ten thousand times!

Obviously, the worst thing about getting injured in WWE is you're sidelined. Being out of action is hard for any WWE performer to deal with.

But one silver lining is that it gives you time to think. To ponder your future. To wonder how you might improve, whether in the ring or in your storytelling.

I decided during my time off that when I finally came back, my future would need to change in a big way. What happened next for Kane would prove to be the most radical evolution in the history of that character.

CHAPTER 8

KANE UNMASKED

One of the most memorable Kane moments occurred in 2002, when I teamed up with Hulk Hogan and The Rock to take on a re-formed New World Order.

On *Raw* one night, Hulk and Rock were seen backstage discussing whether I could be trusted. I eventually joined the two and asked The Rock if he was ready for our match. Rock replied, "You bet—"

"*It doesn't matter if you're ready!*" I interrupted, mimicking The Rock's famous catchphrase. Even though I was backstage, I could hear the crowd explode. "Because tonight, The Rock and Kane team up with Hulk Hogan," I said, doing my best Rock impression.

Then I switched to mimicking Hogan. "And you know something, brothers! Whether it's the millions ["*And millions!*" the crowd repeated] and millions of Rock fans! Or twenty thousand Hulkamaniacs! Or twenty thousand screaming Kaneinites!" Everyone popped for the "Kaneinites."

"The question is, brothers—Scott Hall, Kevin Nash,

X-Pac—*whatcha gonna do* when Hulk Hogan, and The Rock and the Big Red Machine *run wild on you*?" Then I began flexing and cupping my ear just like Hogan. The crowd ate it up.

We might never again see two stars as big as Hulk Hogan and The Rock in sports entertainment.

To say that was a special moment would be an understatement.

Around that time, during a match with X-Pac, I tore my bicep and was out for four months. That was when I began thinking seriously about whether it was time for Kane to lose the mask.

The Face of Kane

Kane's mask had always been an integral part of the character. When I returned from my injury, we transitioned from the original full mask to a mouthless one that showed part of my face. The idea with the mouthless mask was to have something that looked more like a superhero.

Still, my favorite incarnation of the mask will always be the first one. It was the most mysterious, and with my face completely covered, it ensured that no one knew what Kane was thinking.

When I returned, the Kane character was really hot. I had great tag team runs with Hurricane (Gregory Helms) and Rob Van Dam and even ended up winning the Intercontinental Title.

But I wasn't happy. Some creative decisions made during that time did not sit well with me. Kane was red-hot, but I thought creative was squandering it. It was one of the most frustrating times of my career.

At that point, I felt like the mask had become more of a hindrance than an asset. In my mind, it had lost its mystique.

And, while the mask had served its purpose for a time, there was another important reason I wanted to lose it: A WWE performer's greatest asset is his or her face. It's how we show emotion. It's how we help tell stories. You can have the best body or do the most spectacular moves in the world, but when you take away someone's ability to show facial expressions, you handicap them.

I went to Vince with this. We sat down in Dallas, where I told him about my frustrations: that I didn't know exactly which way to go with Kane; and that I thought it was time to get rid of the mask.

Vince said he felt the same way. That was important because only two people in the entire company felt that way— Glenn Jacobs and Vince McMahon. Everyone else had an "If it ain't broke, don't fix it" attitude. They pointed out that Kane with the mask drew money. They weren't wrong.

Vince and I were the only ones willing to take a risk. If it didn't work, I could just put the mask back on. Rey Mysterio reached his greatest popularity ever in WWE with a mask after having worked without a mask in WCW. It's not like unmasking and potentially remasking was unheard of in our business.

My unmasking went down in Madison Square Garden

in June 2003. I fought Triple H for his World Title with the stipulation that if I lost, I would have to unmask. After a lot of interference by Evolution members Randy Orton and Ric Flair, Hunter hit me with his finishing maneuver, the Pedigree, and I lost the match.

That's when *Raw* general manager Eric Bischoff walked out. "Kane, you know the stipulations and you gave your word," Bischoff said. "Now take that mask off!"

I was moving reluctantly to take off my mask when Evolution jumped me. Then my former tag team partner, Rob Van Dam, ran in to help me fight off Triple H, Orton, and Flair. I Chokeslammed Orton, and Rob hit him with the Five-Star Frog Splash.

After we cleared the ring of Evolution, I began to raise my arms upward to make the flames shoot up as I usually did, but paused as Van Dam looked on. I teased, moving to take my mask off a few times, without doing it.

Then, I finally did it. I stopped in the middle of the ring, pulled off my mask, and snapped my head around quickly to face the hard cam, revealing my face—covered with black, sooty makeup—and my half-shaven head. "Oh, my God!" Jerry Lawler yelled.

Then I picked up Rob Van Dam and Chokeslammed him, betraying my friend.

And, just like that, a new era began for Kane.

I was nervous that night. This was a monumental change for my character. I remember Hunter came up to me before the match, reassuring me it would be good. He told me he knew I was going to do a great job and that we should just go out and have fun. Hunter's vote of confidence made me more confident.

Earlier in the day, when I arrived at Madison Square Garden, WWE's longtime hair and makeup person Janet Ventriglia started shearing my head. I told Crystal to watch the show that night, but I didn't tell her why. My wife has always loved me having long hair, so I left out the gory details about what would happen later. To say the least, she wasn't thrilled with my new look.

As Jan continued to shave my head, Bruce Prichard walked in and suggested that we shave only half my head. He said we had a lot of bald guys on the roster, but no one with hair just in the back. I went along with it, but I should have let Jan shave my entire head right then.

I eventually told Vince I couldn't walk around all the time with a half-shaved head because I felt and looked ridiculous. I told him I was just going to shave it all off. That happened the next night in Poughkeepsie, New York, as I was on the way to my first match as unmasked Kane. I was driving with Stevie Richards and referee Charles Robinson, whom many fans will remember as "Little Naitch" during his program with Ric Flair in WCW. We bought some battery-operated clippers, and I let Charles shave the rest of my head. Charles is a hair expert. Just look at him. Does any man in WWE have better hair than Little Naitch?

In some ways, I missed having hair, but in other ways, I didn't. For one thing, my hair would always get tangled up in my mask. I spent half my time in the shower untangling my hair. Now I didn't have a mask or hair anymore! It was great! It was not only better for personal hygiene, but now my showers lasted a mere fraction of the time that they used to.

Rob Van Dam was obviously a big part of my unmasking, as we had been working together as a tag team for six months prior. Even though I kept beating Rob up, he tried to be there for Kane in my time of despair. I even Chokeslammed Rob twice my first night back without the mask in Poughkeepsie. Now that's a true friend!

Rob is a super-talented guy who had a lot to do with me getting over this particular incarnation of Kane.

So did Jim Ross, WWE's longtime wrestling commentator. One of the things many remember most about this time—besides my unmasking—is the interview I did with J.R. just two weeks later.

Setting Good Ol' J.R. on Fire!

As I sat in the chair, with a towel on my head to cover my face, I gave Jim a gift-wrapped package. He opened it to find a gasoline can. I then warned him, "You make fun of me one time during this interview, and I will set you on fire!" Then, I slammed the gasoline can on the table.

Now, most interviewers probably wouldn't have continued with a can of gasoline just sitting there, but hey, this is WWE! I had already gotten physical with Steve Austin because I thought he was making fun of me. I had even Chokeslammed

Raw general manager Eric Bischoff near the entrance ramp for the same reason. Poor Eric broke his thumb as a result.

But J.R. told me he was not there to make fun of me; that I was one of the most extraordinary athletes WWE had ever seen. He showed the footage of Kane destroying Austin and Bischoff.

J.R. then asked what I felt when I saw those images.

"Anger. Hatred," I said.

J.R. asked why.

"J.R., I was a normal, happy child, until a fire turned me into a hideous monster," I said. I asked J.R. why Rob Van Dam and Austin and all my supposed friends so badly wanted everyone to see "my burned face."

"Kane, I'm not quite sure how to put this to you," J.R. said gently. "You wear that towel over your head to hide these horrible marks and burns on your head, but the few times we've seen you without it, you don't appear to be scarred or deformed in any way."

"What are you saying, J.R.?" I shot back. "I was burned. I was in a fire! The fire tore the flesh from my skin!

"You sound just like those doctors from when I was a kid," I continued. "The ones who tried to tell me that those burn marks were only superficial. The ones who wanted me to go see a shrink! All they wanted me to do was to show my face so they could make fun of me.

"So I had to hurt them. *All* of them!" I said ominously. "Look at me, J.R.!" I pulled the towel off my head. "I'm a monster! Don't you see that?"

This was straight out of the novel *Red Dragon*, whose main

character produced much of my inspiration for this incarnation of Kane, now dubbed The Big Red Monster. When I first took off my mask, many had wondered, "I thought Kane was supposed to be burned!"

But Kane wasn't horribly scarred. That was the point. Like the protagonist in *Red Dragon*, who had convinced himself he was hideous, my scars were all in my head. My scars were mental and psychological. There was no sane reason for me to wear a mask, but you couldn't tell Kane that.

J.R. tried in our interview, but I was convinced he was just making fun of me—and he would pay the price.

"Kane, you know what I see?" J.R. said. "I see a man that needs help."

I got in J.R.'s face and screamed, "You need to feel my pain!" I snatched J.R. up by his collar and knocked him out, leaving his body flat on the floor. I took the gasoline and poured it all over him.

Then I took the matches and lit J.R. on fire. You could hear him screaming.

The funny part about all this was that the man burning on the floor was a stuntman. J.R. was still in the room screaming off camera. It was enough to make anyone who could see the whole scene laugh, but the Big Red Monster stayed in character and kept a straight face.

Kane had taken another victim, but there was no way we would have ever actually put J.R. in harm's way.

The same was true for Linda McMahon.

Tombstoning Linda McMahon

Just one week after setting J.R. on fire, Kane gave Linda a Tombstone piledriver on the steel floor of the entrance ramp. Being emotionally unstable and psychotic, I was going after everyone.

I'll never forget when we were rehearsing that angle, I told Linda and everyone else that this was not going to be a textbook Tombstone. There was no way she was going to come anywhere close to getting dropped on her head! Her safety was my paramount concern.

Vince told me that the only two people he would ever trust to do such an outrageous stunt—piledriving his wife—were me and Undertaker.

During rehearsal, I told everyone around me—especially the camera crew—not to shoot the piledriver directly, but to shoot it from a different angle. I told them that I was going to make sure that Linda's head missed the floor by a good two feet or more. I would never take any real chances with her safety.

After we did that angle, I went backstage and, of course, Linda was fine. Everything had gone smoothly.

The same could not be said for the camera crew. Unfortunately, when I set Linda up for the Tombstone and dropped her, the cameras didn't cut away quickly enough. They caught the move head-on, and it was obvious to viewers that Linda's head was nowhere near the floor when she landed.

Backstage, Vince was livid. You could see in his face that he was mad. Not at me, but at the production crew.

I sat by Vince but quickly moved away. I had done my part, but didn't want to be anywhere near Vince, who was still fuming at the botched camera work.

Kane's Favorite Pastime: Torturing Shane McMahon

The following week, in Colorado Springs, Vince was still mad at *Raw*, but this time as part of the story line. "I'm here on *Raw* tonight for one reason and one reason only, and that's to avenge what Kane did last week to my wife, Linda," Vince said. "I came here to confront Kane, not because I'm a good husband, hell, everybody here tonight knows better than that. I'm here to confront Kane because I'm *the man* and Kane's not!

"Kane's not a man at all. Kane is an animal!" Vince continued. I was supposed to be under house arrest for what I had done to Linda. Instead, Vince announced, "I have summoned the authorities to present Kane to me here tonight in that very ring." He promised the audience that before the night was over, "all hell will break loose!"

And it did. What happened next is probably my all-time favorite Kane vignette.

A sheriff's van pulled in backstage. *Raw* general manager Eric Bischoff instructed the police officers that Kane was to remain locked inside the "paddy wagon" until he got the word directly from Mr. McMahon to release me.

When they finally opened the doors, I emerged in chains,

Hannibal Lecter style. I loved it. I thought to myself, "This is how Kane should come out every night!" It was tremendous.

Still shackled, I descended into the ring to confront Vince, who got up in my face and said that it would be "too easy to beat the hell out of me" with the chains on. He ordered the officers to remove them and then dismissed the officers.

Turning to me, he asked who I thought I was to beat up a McMahon. Then he got personal. "Who do you think you are?" he repeated mockingly. "Some sort of French-fried freak? Some sort of Frankenstein?

"Yeah, you know what?" Vince continued. "Maybe you are. But then again, I know who you are. You're a..." Vince paused. "You're a monster. You're a real, live, remorseless monster.

"And what would a man like me do with a monster in the palm of his hand?" Vince asked himself. Everyone could see where this was going. Vince grinned widely. "I mean. I could almost forgive you for what you did to my wife so long as the ends justify the means."

The mind of the evil Mr. McMahon was working feverishly. "So imagine this—McMahon and Kane! That has a nice ring to it!"

Just a few days after I had assaulted his wife, Mr. McMahon was more concerned with how he could use me to further his own devious agenda. He had a new toy in me. That became his priority, not seeking justice for what I did to Linda.

You just gotta love Vince!

Steve Austin, who was acting as co–general manager with Bischoff, came down to the ring to interrupt Kane and

Mr. McMahon and tried to provoke me into a fight. Austin's managerial role did not allow him to touch WWE Superstars otherwise. He did everything he could to get me to hit him, but I refused to take the bait.

Then Shane McMahon, Vince and Linda's son, showed up. Shane immediately charged me, sending us both over the top rope. Shane went wild on me, fists flying, seeking revenge for what I had done to his mother. Vince pulled Shane off of me. Mr. McMahon didn't want Shane damaging his prized property. That was when Mr. McMahon got knocked out by his own son!

I tried to escape by running up the ramp, but Shane chased me down and began hitting me with a steel chair. He eventually knocked me off the stage, sending me crashing through tables. *Raw* ended that night with me sitting amid the table debris, laughing maniacally.

I was an unstoppable monster—and the now infamous rivalry between Kane and Shane had begun.

Where do we even start?

Shane and I had so many memorable moments. How can anyone forget our Last Man Standing match at *Unforgiven* in 2003 in Hershey, Pennsylvania? I won, but only because Shane tried to jump on me from the top of the TitanTron, and I moved.

On *Raw* in Tucson, Arizona, we brawled all over backstage until I had Shane knocked out cold on the loading docks outside the arena. I poured cans of gasoline into a dumpster and even threw the cans into it to make the flames even more ferocious. When I got ready to send Shane into the flames of hell, he turned it around and pushed me into the fire!

There was our Ambulance Match at *Survivor Series 2003* in Dallas, Texas, where Shane hit me with the Coast-to-Coast dive from the roof of the ambulance. I Tombstoned him on the concrete floor and then threw him into the ambulance for the win.

Night after night, Shane would do the craziest stunts. He's an adrenaline junkie and really loves being a daredevil, something you can see whenever he's in the ring.

During that time, I remember being beaten half to death by Shane, who was wielding a thin, hollow piece of wood called a kendo stick, in a series of hardcore matches. I was at the gym one day, and some guy saw all the marks on my back and said, "Man, I don't know what happened to you, but you should be in a lot of pain." I was!

One night, as Shane was wailing on me with the kendo stick, I decided I'd had enough. I returned fire, to let him know how bad it hurt, and he was like, "*Whoa*, sorry!" He immediately got the message.

But Shane could take any beating you gave him. He's one of the toughest guys in the locker room and he's not even technically a wrestler. Everyone respects him for what he's willing to put his body through.

My next big program was with Undertaker. With Kane unmasked, it was a completely fresh rivalry. I was in main events throughout this entire era. It was a great time to be Kane.

Which taught me an important lesson. While I had been frustrated with my career right before I ditched the mask, almost to the point of quitting, I would never again find myself in that kind of negative headspace.

It's a funny thing about the wrestling business. When you feel that your career is in a lull or even that your character is past the point of no return, a switch can be flicked and, just like that, you're back on top. I'm not saying this is the case with every wrestler, but it happens more often than performers acknowledge and fans realize.

Early in their careers, wrestlers may not be mature enough or experienced enough to understand this. But if they stick it out, they begin to understand that all of this is cyclical.

You never know what might come next in this business.

Kane could even become a comedian!

CHAPTER 9

TEAM HELL NO

I once asked my trainer, the wrestling legend Boris Malenko, if he preferred singles or tag team wrestling. He said it depends on whom you're working with. In singles, obviously, your opponent matters. With tag teams, your partner definitely matters.

No one could ask for a better partner than Daniel Bryan.

Team Hell No was the most fun I've ever had in my career. If X-Pac helped bring out a more human side to the Big Red Machine, Daniel Bryan helped bring out a more comedic side.

While I have played a dark character most of my career, I'm actually laid-back, easygoing, and pretty upbeat most of the time. Anyone who knows me would likely tell you the same thing.

So, in real life, I'm basically the opposite of Kane! The Kane who fans saw team with Daniel Bryan was closer to Glenn Jacobs than anything else I had ever done with that character.

When the idea first arose for Team Hell No, I was sitting in a production meeting. The writers were talking about maybe pairing Bryan and me together as sort of a misfit tag team. Then Road Dogg warned that, if everyone wasn't careful, WWE might end up with a great new babyface tag team.

That was exactly what happened.

"Anger Management" with Dr. Shelby

I had been in a story line with both Daniel Bryan and CM Punk that led to a match between Bryan and me at *Summer-Slam* in 2012.

He beat me with a small package, and afterward I went backstage searching for him, angry and upset. Cameras showed me stomping down the halls, throwing anything I could get my hands around, while everyone ran away in fear. I snatched interviewer Josh Mathews up and screamed, "*Where is he?*" in his face before tossing him aside.

That match and the aftermath were the beginning of our pairing.

Bryan and I already knew we would become a tag team before *SummerSlam*. We had been recording vignettes with our "therapist," "Dr. Shelby," who was helping both of us work on "anger management" issues.

Those therapy sessions were a lot of fun. Bryan and I continued to go at each other, while Dr. Shelby did all he could to keep the peace. Our characters were so full of themselves that, in one segment on *SmackDown*, Daniel said to me, "And speaking of doing things wrong, why don't we talk about what happened on Monday night?"

I stood up, so we were face-to-face. "I did what I had to do to be victorious," I told Bryan point-blank. "I want to be the next tag team champion!"

Notice I said "champion"—singular, not plural, as you might expect with a tag team.

Bryan replied, "I want to be the next tag team champion," which was also singular.

I parroted the same line back. I even wore a shirt once, after we actually won the tag titles, that read, "I am the tag team champions." It was all about me!

This was a running gag. We were completely dysfunctional.

Many fans remember those Dr. Shelby skits fondly. Probably the most memorable was our reenactment of the famous diner scene from the movie *When Harry Met Sally*. As our food was placed on the table in front of us, Dr. Shelby said, "I want you each to take one bite. To feel how the other feels. Walk a mile in his shoes."

In this therapy experiment, our food had been switched around. In front of me was just a salad, which was what strict vegan Daniel Bryan would eat. But Bryan had a plate of meatballs, a meal more suitable for Kane and no doubt repugnant to Daniel.

After I ate a bite, Dr. Shelby asked, "Kane, how do you feel?" I belched loudly in his face.

"Daniel, how do you feel?" he asked Bryan, who had just eaten a meatball.

"It wasn't as bad as I thought," Bryan replied. Then he got sick in Dr. Shelby's lap.

I just laughed and said, "Check, please!"

We taped that vignette in Albany, New York, at an actual diner. I remember the other customers looking at us. We had our own room for filming, but most of the patrons could still see us. They must have been thinking, "What in the heck is this?"

In another segment, Bryan and I were sitting in a group therapy session and Dr. Shelby asked, "So tell us, Kane, what makes you angry?" The camera shot pulled back to include both Bryan and me. "Please, Kane, we're here to help, so maybe start from your childhood?" Dr. Shelby added. "Remember, sharing is caring."

Bryan just put his head in his hands and said, "This is a bad idea."

As the camera slowly zoomed in on me, I did exactly what Dr. Shelby had asked me to do.

Kane shared his childhood!

"I grew up locked in a basement," I began. "Suffering severe psychological and emotional scarring when my brother set my parents on fire. From there, I shifted around among a series of mental institutions until I was grown, at which point, I buried my brother alive. Twice."

Bryan still had his head buried in his hands. The woman sitting next to me looked at me like I was insane. I was just getting started. "Since then, I've set a couple of people on fire, and abducted various coworkers," I added.

It kept getting better—or worse? "My real father is a guy named Paul Bearer who I recently trapped in a meat locker,"

I continued. "I've been married, divorced. Broke up my ex-wife's wedding and Tombstoned a priest. And, for reasons never quite explained, I have an unhealthy obsession with torturing Pete Rose."

Everyone in the room looked shocked. "Okay, maybe we should call it a day," Dr. Shelby said. My summary of Kane's actual story lines over the years was downright hilarious in that setting.

It was great.

The actor who played Dr. Shelby, Michael Aspinwall, was also a high school teacher based out of Los Angeles. He is a really nice guy, and Bryan and I had a lot of fun with him. From what I understand, his students thought his regular appearances on WWE television showed that he was pretty cool.

WWE brought Dr. Shelby back in 2018 to help ease tensions between quarreling friends Sasha Banks and Bayley, who were forced into counseling by *Raw* general manager Kurt Angle.

Those vignettes were important for Team Hell No. It's often more constructive to have fewer televised matches and expand story lines in other creative ways. Sometimes, when match follows match, they get lost. But when you craft a vignette that's entertaining, fans remember it.

"Team Hell No"? What About "Team Friendship"?!

Team Hell No developed at a time when WWE was focusing more on fan interaction through social media. One night on *Raw*, fans were asked through a Twitter poll, "What do you want Daniel Bryan and Kane to do tonight?" The choices were "Compete against each other," "Compete as a tag team," or "Hug it out."

Not surprisingly, 55 percent chose "Hug it out." Bryan and I approached each other reluctantly in the ring. He hesitantly put his arms around me, but I didn't hug back. He started screaming, "You didn't hug me! You didn't *hug me*!" It was hard not to laugh. I loved it.

By this point, the crowd was getting pretty loud. Wrestling commentator Michael Cole said, "All of the 13,604 are chanting 'Hug him back' as #WWEHUG trends worldwide on Twitter!"

Arms outstretched, I approached Daniel. It must have looked comical. The Demon going in for a warm hug! "This is one of the most bizarre moments that I've ever witnessed," Cole said.

When we finally got to the big hug, the crowd ate it up. Of course, right after that, we started slapping each other around again, but that was the beauty of Team Hell No.

Which probably makes it a good time to discuss something few people know. Bryan and I never wanted our name to be Team Hell No. WWE allowed fans to choose our name via a Twitter poll, which included the one Bryan and I had our hearts set on: Team Friendship.

We even had shirts picked out that were to have carried the team name! We thought kids would like it. It was over the top, babyface.

When fans chose Team Hell No instead, both of us were like, "Aghh, we can't put that on a kid's shirt!"

"YES!" "NO!"

But the whole thing gelled really well. We loved it. The fans loved it. Prior to Team Hell No, it had always been hard for Kane to interact with the audience. Kane never cut long DX-style promos or had catchphrases like Steve Austin or The Rock. It was the first time I got to do something like this.

Many fans remember that Bryan and I would often scream "Yes!" and "No!" back and forth to each other, a riff on his original "Yes!" movement catchphrase. I remember, after doing this one night, walking to the back and hearing Dean Malenko say, "I've never seen anything like that. People are cheering and booing both of you, even though you're on the same team!"

I think our teaming really helped us both. It showed fans I could do something besides behave in a sinister fashion.

As for Bryan, it helped him spin off into even more singles success, which elevated him further.

One funny story I remember was when WWE was in Russia on my forty-sixth birthday, in 2013. We had a show in Moscow where Kane, Daniel Bryan, and John Cena took on Big E, Dolph Ziggler, and Ryback.

After the match, as I was about to leave the ring, Cena led the audience in singing "Happy Birthday" to me. Everyone had a Russian accent! Then they put a Russian hat on my head. They made me close my eyes and asked me to stick out my right hand. Bryan put a banana in it. I was like, "What?"

They told me to close my eyes again. Then Bryan and John just left the ring. When they got backstage, John asked Bryan what they were going to do next. Bryan said to just leave me out there. John said, "We can't do that! We have a plane to catch!"

We always had a good time. Everything we did, people laughed, no matter how ridiculous the idea. It always worked because of the nature of our team. I really enjoyed being light-hearted with my character, for a change.

"Green" Daniel Bryan

Daniel Bryan is a really good guy. One of the best people in the world. As of this writing, he's walking around as WWE Champion with an organic title made out of wood and hemp, berating the fans for not being environmentally conscious enough.

Guess what? That's really him!

That's not a character. In real life, Bryan might not be a jerk about it, as he is on television, but every "green" word that comes out of his mouth genuinely reflects his deeply held beliefs.

I remember one time, when he was on the WWE brand known as NXT, the producers were making the wrestlers undertake various challenges. This was before NXT was the brand it is today, but rather a weekly reality competition to determine the next "breakout Superstar." Bryan was challenged to sell as many programs as he could to the audience. He had all these programs in his hand. At one point, he was like, "Gosh, I'm not a capitalist. What am I doing?" He just started handing the programs out to people.

I couldn't help but think, "Not a capitalist? He works for a company that is in the business of making money. He's making money right now! It's what we do every day!"

Bryan isn't really a socialist. He's just very concerned about the environment. He's really open-minded. I shared with him some books by libertarian icon and former congressman Ron Paul, R-Texas (more on him later), and writings by former Libertarian presidential candidate Harry Browne.

Like Bryan, I too care about the environment. Everyone should. I just get concerned when politicians and activists try to use the environment to push overregulation and bigger government, which they always do.

Many people think "capitalism" means people can do whatever they like, without worrying about the consequences to the environment or anything else. That's not the case. If the government were to enforce property rights—which it doesn't—problems like pollution would be solved more easily. No one has the right to pollute my property—or anyone else's. Government is supposed to hold accountable those who infringe on others' rights or contracts.

I'm even in agreement, in principle, with many of the Green Party's positions. My concern is that I don't think many realize what kind of authoritarianism would be required to enforce the Green Party's vision.

Historically, as societies become more affluent through capitalism, they begin to care about issues like the environment and begin to seek solutions. When people are poor, surviving day to day, as has been the case in many socialist countries, people don't really care about the environment. They don't have the time or resources to do so. They're too busy just trying to get by.

Even though Bryan and I have our differences—on the political spectrum we're probably about as far apart as two people could be—he respects where I'm coming from and I respect where he's coming from. He's one of the most respected people in the locker room, and we've been good friends since day one.

We can do that because when we discuss political issues, we do so in a nonconfrontational way. We are both coming from good places. We both want a better world for our friends and family.

Now that I think about it, Team Hell No might be a good blueprint for better political dialogue on the national level! Bryan and I have always discussed politics and just about everything else diplomatically.

That's what we need to start doing as a country!

Daniel Bryan's Biggest Fan

When concussions and other injuries forced Bryan to temporarily retire in 2014, I was heartbroken. He had worked so hard—harder than anyone could possibly imagine—to get where he was, and then it was all taken away from him. It reminded me of the time I blew out my knee playing football. You work so feverishly every day of your life to achieve your dreams and then, one day, you're done.

To fall from the heights of what Jerry Lawler called "YEStleMania!" into retirement was too much for Bryan to take.

WWE management does everything it can to protect the health of its employees. Sometimes people think Vince is cold-hearted or doesn't care, a point of view that his character certainly supports.

But it's not remotely true. In Bryan's case, the company was being as cautious as it could—and should—have been! Nothing is more important than your health.

Especially in the sports entertainment business.

I was the happiest person in the world that day in March 2018 when Bryan was cleared to return to the ring. I'm the biggest Daniel Bryan fan around. That was a great day for him and the entire WWE Universe.

It was a great day for me, too.

CHAPTER 10

CORPORATE KANE

Around the time the idea for Corporate Kane began germinating, I had just finished shooting the sequel to my horror movie *See No Evil* in Vancouver. Though I had grown my hair long again, I had to shave my head for the movie.

It wasn't a huge deal, but I wasn't happy about cutting my hair again!

During that time, I was supposed to get a slight break, something WWE performers rarely get. Instead, I ended up spending my entire "break" shooting the movie. Such is life.

I must admit, it was much less grueling than trying to avoid a volcano, though.

Burned Out

The movie was a lot of work, but I had a great time on the set. The famed horror directors and producers Jen and Sylvia Soska—aka "the Soska Twins"—were a thrill to work with.

But my travel schedule the week the movie wrapped was no thrill. Two days before I finished the movie, I get a call from WWE asking me to travel to Kansas City to shoot a commercial for the *Royal Rumble*. This would prove to be difficult because I didn't have any of my wrestling gear with me.

My Kane costume was back home in Tennessee; I had been busy playing my other evil character, Jacob Goodnight!

I got the call from WWE on a Thursday night. The shoot was on Monday. I wrapped up the movie on Saturday, and flew that day to New York City to participate in Comic Con.

That night, I was supposed to fly back home to Knoxville to get my wrestling gear, stay overnight, then fly Sunday to Kansas City for the shoot.

That's a lot of traveling—even if everything goes smoothly, right? Of course, things did not go smoothly.

While en route to the airport in New York City that Saturday, intending to travel to Knoxville, I told the driver that I hated flying out of LaGuardia. It's a small, compact airport and it has just two runways. If one goes down, you're done. If both are out of commission, obviously, you're not going anywhere. In the past decade, I've been stranded overnight at least three times at LaGuardia because I couldn't get a flight out.

That day, I arrived at LaGuardia four hours early. I thought I was good. Of course, being LaGuardia, my flight was delayed. I was connecting in Philadelphia and was told that I would still make my flight to Knoxville, despite the delay. When I got off the plane in Philly, I was met by an airline representative. I thought he was there to expedite me to the gate so I could catch my connecting flight.

No, he was there to tell me I was stuck in Philly. My flight had already left. There were no other flights available.

I'd had it. That's when I called Mark Carrano.

Mark is the head of Talent Relations for WWE. He could tell I was frustrated. I told him this whole ad shoot wasn't even my idea! He put me on the phone with Cathy Morrell, who handles WWE's travel scheduling. Mark warned Cathy, "This is not the Glenn you're used to dealing with."

Cathy is a true professional and great at her job. She looked through all the options and none of them were good. I ended up renting a car and driving nine hours home. Otherwise, I would have had to jump off a plane in Knoxville the next day, grab my gear from Crystal at the airport, and then jump back onto another plane, praying I got to Kansas City on time.

At that point, I didn't have much faith that the airlines would come through, even if I had chosen that route.

But that wasn't all. On top of all that travel craziness, I had to fly out of Kansas City to Washington, where I had scheduled political stops with some prominent activist groups.

Remember, this was all in a span of four days!

My first stop in Washington was at the offices of the conservative and libertarian advocacy group FreedomWorks. I didn't know what to think when I arrived, my head kind of fuzzy from all the traveling, but when I saw posters supporting Ron Paul, the political public figure most responsible for inspiring me to get into politics, I felt right at home. It proved to be a nice, short break from the all-consuming worlds of movies and wrestling.

I made a few other stops that day, including one at the

headquarters of the Heritage Foundation. There, I attended a roundtable discussion with experts about free-market economics and property rights. After the meeting adjourned, some attendees wanted to get a picture with me. I was happy to oblige. Then, a small line formed in the hallway for more photo ops. It became a mini Kane meet and greet!

For those who don't know, the Heritage Foundation is one of Washington's oldest conservative think tanks, having risen to prominence during the Reagan administration. It is also home to more than a few wrestling fans, as I learned that day! I always knew that the WWE Universe reaches far and wide, but it is nice when little things along the way remind me just how expansive it is.

This was something some of my critics didn't seem to understand when I decided to run for mayor. My sports entertainment background was a novelty for many, but never in a negative way. It helped me get press and publicity most conventional candidates couldn't get. Today, with the exception of the mayors of major cities like New York City, Los Angeles, and Chicago, no other mayor in the country can get the national television exposure that I can.

But, while that kind of attention due to my WWE celebrity set me apart during the campaign, it didn't get me elected. Instead, it merely opened the door with voters. The people put me in office because they liked what I had to say.

Before I was elected, many political "experts" predicted that my pro-wrestling career would prove to be a handicap. I knew there was the potential for that, but I also knew it could be my greatest asset if I played it right.

I mean, here I was in the nation's capital to talk politics with leaders of one of the world's most prestigious conservative think tanks—and I ended up taking photos with Kane fans!

I have recounted my hectic travel schedule on the week that Corporate Kane came into being to drive home an important point: I was burned out. I used to think artists who talked about being burned out were silly or melodramatic. Then it happened to me.

When you're good or successful at something in whatever field you choose, you are likely to want to do it for as long as you can.

But, no matter how enjoyable you may find it, eventually you will want to do something else. At this point, Team Hell No was essentially done, and I was back to being the same dark monster I had portrayed for nearly two decades.

As with Team Hell No, it was time for another change.

What If Kane Became Triple H's Henchman?

Triple H and I came up with the idea. I wanted to be Hunter's henchman. He further molded that concept into what would become Corporate Kane.

I didn't like the name. I thought I should just be Kane, but with a new gimmick. To me, the gimmick would speak for itself. Vince felt like there needed to be some name differentiation from the Big Red Monster, and so Corporate Kane it was.

Kane's next metamorphosis would be no different. I was

originally supposed to be two distinct characters. Corporate Kane was never supposed to wrestle. I was just supposed to be The Authority guy, who would do promos and generally act like a jerk. Yet, when The Authority had a problem, Hunter or Stephanie would pull out the mask, hand it to me, and those problems would be solved. Eventually, we would plan for Kane to keep the mask.

Corporate Kane would be like The Great Muta, of Japanese wrestling and WCW fame, who was always switching back and forth between his real name, Keiji Mutoh, and his mystical Muta character.

It would also be similar to Sting in WCW, who went from the bleach-blond surfer gimmick to his dark persona reminiscent of Brandon Lee's character in *The Crow*.

A good comparison in today's WWE would be Finn Balor, who transforms into The Demon King to intimidate and vanquish his rivals.

Another concept I had with this new shift in Kane's character was that I would be corrupted by my hunger for power. What's more evil than wanting to achieve more power by hurting as many people as you can?

What lies behind the veneer of the rich and mighty? What does it do to people when they seize power? What kind of psychopath yearns to control others?

On paper, Corporate Kane could have been the most psychopathic version of my character to date!

I think about this all the time in politics. As a libertarian, I'm constantly amazed that while few people say they are satisfied with government leaders, many appear eager to give them more power. They apparently believe that the same flawed figures they don't like will somehow magically improve themselves and society if we just give them more of what they already can't handle. It doesn't make sense.

Most politicians promise to fix what's wrong with the country by giving even more power to government. Does it ever occur to them that many of the problems we have might be due to government already having too much power?

Director of Operations

One of my favorite times as Corporate Kane, The Authority's "director of operations," was my story line with Daniel Bryan. (Remember what Boris Malenko said about great partners?) Bryan began accusing me of being a sellout by allying with the McMahons; he constantly asked what had happened to the Kane of old. As things escalated, I became so enraged at Bryan that, one night on *Raw*, I came up through a hole in the ring to try to drag his wife, Brie Bella, down into hell with me.

Thankfully, for her, she escaped!

The story climaxed at *Extreme Rules 2014* at the Izod Center in Rutherford, New Jersey, where I fought Bryan for his WWE Championship in the main event. Since it was an Extreme Rules Match, it should not surprise anyone that we ended up fighting backstage, where Bryan began beating me with a snow shovel. Then he punched me in the face while we were both on top of a car, until I slammed him on the hood, breaking the windshield.

But we were just getting started.

After I broke more car windows, first with a chemical tank and then with my fist, Bryan knocked me out with a crowbar. After briefly wondering what to do with my unconscious body, he picked me up with a forklift, drove it into the arena, and dumped my carcass in the ring. Bryan then climbed to the top of the forklift, from where he led the entire audience in a "Yes!" chant. The crowd loved it.

Bryan then jumped off the forklift and hit me with a flying headbutt. He went for the cover to pin me. "1-2...*No!*" I popped up. It was the first of many near falls.

Still, how much crazier could this match get?

I tried to Tombstone Bryan on a steel chair, but he reversed it, hitting me with a DDT instead. He tried hitting me with a kendo stick, attempted a suicide dive, and then repeatedly walloped me with the same chair. None of it worked. He even put me in the "Yes!" lock with the kendo stick. That didn't work, either. I broke the hold.

That was when I Chokeslammed him through the announce table. After that, I pulled out a table, poured gasoline all over it, and lit it on fire. He was done for.

Until Bryan put me through the table instead! "The Demon's burning in hell!" screamed Michael Cole.

The audience was on their feet. No one knew what to expect next. This match could go either way. When I made it back into the ring, Bryan hit me with a knee to the face, and that was all she wrote.

Daniel Bryan had defeated Kane to retain his WWE Title.

That match and the rest of our entire Authority saga

marked a great time for me. That story with Bryan remains one of my favorite memories during my run as Corporate Kane.

Burning It Down with Seth Rollins

Another highlight occurred when I turned against Seth Rollins. Most fans remember when Seth betrayed The Shield, the popular three-man faction he formed with Roman Reigns and Dean Ambrose, to join The Authority. That piece of business led Seth and me to find ourselves beholden to the authoritarian McMahon family, both of us playing heels.

Seth kept challenging my role as director of operations within the faction, even questioning my sanity. One night, in the ring on *Raw*, an "expert" declared me to be of "sound mind"—that is, perfectly capable of carrying out my professional duties within The Authority. Afterward, Seth came out and beat me with a chair so badly that I was put into an ambulance to be taken to a hospital.

Well, the ambulance only made it a few feet. As Seth held up his WWE Title in the ring and bragged about his dominance after having beaten me down, the backstage cameras once again focused on the ambulance. As both the fans and Seth stared at the TitanTron to see what might happen, the doors swung open, smoke came pouring out the back—and the Demon Kane appeared!

"Oh, my God," Michael Cole exclaimed, adding, "Run, Seth, Run!"

I returned to the ring and brutalized Rollins until he scurried away. The segment ended with flames shooting up from the four corners of the ring as I held Seth's title high in the air.

Unfortunately for Kane, our story would end at *Hell in a Cell 2015*, where Seth retained his championship and I was ultimately fired as The Authority's director of operations.

That run with Seth was one of the best moments during my time as Corporate Kane. Working with Seth was always a blast, and I have the utmost respect for him. He's an amazing performer. Few, if any, of the top talents of the current WWE can hold a candle to Seth Rollins.

Corporate Problems

Unfortunately, a lot of the plans for Corporate Kane got muddled more than Hunter or I had planned. For me, the original plan was that Corporate Kane would be a straight-laced company shill, and Demon Kane would emerge from time to time to kick butt and handle The Authority's business.

Sometimes, that was the way it did play out, as the story with Seth makes clear. But, once Corporate Kane began to wrestle, fans had a tough time understanding what was going on. There was no longer a tangible line between the two characters.

Every version of Kane has been a success, and while I had a lot of fun with it and was involved in some pretty memorable moments as Corporate Kane, I'm not sure it measured up to my success with Team Hell No.

But that's par for the course in our business. Even in 2014, when Corporate Kane emerged, WWE story lines were moving so fast that sometimes what we created didn't end up making as much sense as we had intended. Details get lost because you're driving down the road at two hundred miles an hour and you can't see the color of every car you pass.

The hottest time in the history of our business was the Attitude Era, when we were putting together only two hours of prime-time television per week for *Monday Night Raw.*

Fast-forward to today. Now, we have three hours of *Raw*, two hours of *SmackDown*, constant new content for the WWE Network, including *NXT* and specials. We also have more pay-per-views today than we did twenty years ago.

Some people are critical of our creative team, but I often think, "I'd like to see anyone else come up with consistently compelling story lines to fill all that time." It's one thing when you're on the outside looking in. It's quite another when you're working on the inside—nonstop, all day, every day—to deliver a top-notch product.

It's hard to keep up! It's even harder to deliver consistently and ceaselessly.

Believe it not, it was during my time as Corporate Kane that Triple H and I worked together the most, and it was a time that I really enjoyed. We had both been on top for most of the Attitude Era, but our paths didn't cross as much back then.

When it comes to the sports entertainment business, Triple H is a genius. His creativity is unmatched. The NXT brand is a prime example. It began as a farm system for WWE, but has morphed into an enormously popular third brand that continues to produce some of the company's biggest Superstars.

He also excels on the business side of things, as shown by the WWE's Performance Center in Orlando, Florida, a state-of-the-art training facility and Triple H's brainchild.

Talking about my work with Hunter reminds me of his wife, Stephanie McMahon, and one of the more comical stories from the Corporate Kane days.

Stephanie Saves Kane from the Spotlight Flames of Hell

While Kane and "flames of hell!" have often been mentioned in the same breath, let me tell you there's nothing hotter than our stage lights. The lights that make WWE Superstars look so good in the ring are scorching. The lights backstage are just as blistering. They're intolerable.

For *years*, I would plead, "They're killing me with these lights!" And for all those years, those complaints fell on deaf ears. They said, "Suck it up." So I did.

Once, I was shooting a vignette with Stephanie in a room backstage. As usual, I was sweating to death under my Corporate Kane suit. Stephanie said, "It's really hot in here!" I was like, "*Thank you!*"

Stephanie asked the tech guys if there was anything that

could be done about the heat. They said LED lights could alleviate the heat, but they were very expensive.

Guess what? The next week we had LED light boards! The lighting and heat situation immediately improved. Hallelujah!

It pays to be Steph!

Like her dad, Stephanie McMahon is a great performer. In our interactions over the years, she was always straight with me, and a pleasure to work with. Many other WWE performers will tell you the same thing.

I've always had a lot of respect for Steph. She also does a lot of charity work behind the scenes, even more than the public knows. What you see on camera only scratches the surface. Like her husband, Stephanie adds so much to WWE that many don't even realize.

Some fans didn't like Corporate Kane. They thought it was too much of a departure from the traditional character and that I didn't really look like Kane anymore.

But if you want to survive in WWE, especially if you want to stay on top, you have to change. You can't become stale. You have to keep reinventing yourself. In fact, if you are going to remain essentially the same version of a character for any extended period of time, it's better to go away for a while, stay off television and house shows, so that fans don't get tired of you. Many of us have done that.

Still, some of the most successful performers in the modern era of WWE have consistently reinvented themselves.

Look at my brother! You had the original Undertaker, aka Deadman, then the more sinister Ministry of Darkness, followed by American Badass, and then sort of a Deadman-Badass hybrid. When Undertaker appears today, it's with an updated look of the classic character fans fell in love well over two decades ago.

What's old is new again.

Consider the evolution of Shawn Michaels. The one-time Rocker became The Heartbreak Kid as a singles star, who would become even more outrageous as the leader of D-Generation X.

When Shawn returned in 2002, after a four-year hiatus, he was a different man and his character reflected that. His later WWE run is considered by many to be some of the best work of his career, but the "Showstopper" who retired Ric Flair with a Superkick in 2008 was a very different character from the guy who wrestled Razor Ramon in a Ladder Match in 1995.

Triple H is no different. His name comes from his original "Blueblood" aristocrat gimmick, which he used in both WCW and WWE, which evolved into something much edgier when he began running with The Kliq.

The Hunter we later saw in D-Generation X was just as edgy, but with a juvenile delinquent component added.

When Triple H began to establish himself as a top singles competitor, The Game was born, a calculating and merciless character who would eventually lead Evolution along with Ric Flair. Then he became part of the WWE "establishment" as The Authority. When he wrestles today, fans bow down to "The King of Kings."

Do we even have to get into the major transformations that

Hulk Hogan, Kevin Nash, and Scott Hall underwent as they revamped their old WWE characters to lead the New World Order and WCW to nearly two years of ratings dominance? Or how Sting's massive character change played such an integral part in that company's success?

Corporate Kane was a major step in keeping my character fresh, and while I would have set up some of the story arc differently, I loved every minute of it.

CHAPTER II

THE DIFFERENCE BETWEEN WRESTLING AND POLITICS

Political Fans Don't Know That What They're Watching Is Scripted

At some point, every wrestler and every wrestling fan hears that dreaded word: "fake."

I never use this word. Yes, the matches are scripted and the outcomes preplanned, but the effort we put into our craft and the resulting entertainment is as real as anything else.

And there's nothing fake about the toll it takes on your body. I've had too many injuries and aches that linger to this day for anyone to tell me what I do isn't real. I know many in the WWE locker room feel the same way.

I'm often amused by folks who ridicule pro wrestling as

"fake" because so much else that entertains us is "fake" as well.

For example, some who describe sports entertainment as "fake" might also watch television shows where zombies take over the world. The word has been uttered by people who watch action movies where the star magically survives hundreds of rounds of ammunition being fired at him. Some of the same moviegoers who help superhero films rake in billions at the box office might have also been dismissive at some point of sports entertainment's authenticity.

All of these programming examples are fantasy based. Sorry, folks, as much as I love them, too, dragons and wizards aren't real.

The "fake" word is even used on occasion by people who watch "reality" television. Does anyone honestly believe those characters—and they *are* characters—don't behave differently when the cameras are off? Or that they aren't encouraged to do certain things by the producers? Or that their performances might even be scripted?

A reality show that chronicles someone making trips to the grocery store or taking out the trash wouldn't be exciting. These programs take real-life circumstances and manipulate them for maximum entertainment. They want the audience to invest in their characters.

As sports entertainment aficionados might say, they need their stars to "get over."

Trying to elicit an emotional response from people to earn their dollars is nothing new. Shakespeare did it. So does Celine Dion.

The same is true, unfortunately, when it comes to getting votes. All too often, people buy into a persona, not the human being behind it. Politicians are experts at pushing our emotional buttons to get us to push the button next to their name at the ballot box. Sometimes they use fear, other times it's the promise of something for nothing. In either case, they are peddling a fantasy designed to get them elected, not the truth voters need to hear.

I credit my election as mayor of Knox County, Tennessee, in large part to the fact that voters thought I was real. Glenn Jacobs didn't need that job. I told people that. I had no reason to be dishonest with them. I wanted to become mayor because I was passionate about public service. Unlike most politicians, I would always be straight with my constituents.

My authenticity helped me win the election.

Needless to say, it's unusual in our politics.

Democrats and Republicans at all levels of government tell voters exactly what they want to hear about any number of issues, regardless of whether they plan to address those issues if they get elected. They know the right buzzwords to say and the right emotional buttons to push, and they do what they can to get a reaction out of their audience.

It's showbiz.

It's pro wrestling! Name another business besides politics, especially at the national level, where there is an antagonist and a protagonist (which depends on where you stand politically) and the winner is portrayed as having a colossal impact on our lives.

But after every election, does anything really change? To

the degree that it does, is that change ever as radical as what the political doomsayers had predicted? What did the election story line ultimately lead to?

After *WrestleMania*, there is always *Raw* the next night. Life goes on, no matter how consequential the previous night's events might have seemed at the time.

After any election, there's always another. Story lines begin building again.

Just as in sports entertainment, many politicians who fight in public have much different relationships with each other when they are behind closed doors.

It's also true that most conventional Republicans and moderate Democrats—the people who fill that centrist space on the ideological spectrum that provides the votes to elect most presidents—don't differ significantly on many issues.

Look at the suggested income tax rates between the two parties. They usually differ by around three points! A mere three percentage points, and they would have you believe they are worlds apart!

The cults of personality that form around political figures often overshadow the actual issues. Races often become more about personalities than about ideas or policy prescriptions.

It's my team versus your team. But, trust me, folks, you ain't part of anyone's team.

When I ran for mayor, the local political establishment laughed at me. Who did this wrestler think he was? What gave him the *right* to run for mayor? You see, they want you to vote, they want you to support them financially, but they don't want you to join them.

After all, you might want to shake things up.

It gets worse at the national level. The reason that Donald Trump causes so much angst among the political establishment, the elitist cocktail party crowd, is that he's not one of them.

The political class can't control him. As a populist, he doesn't need them. In fact, his political base rejects them.

The same is true on the other side. Why do you think the Democratic National Committee colluded with Hillary Clinton's campaign to deprive Bernie Sanders of their party's presidential nomination in 2016?

Much like Trump is on the Right, Sanders is a populist on the Left.

Both of them, in their own way, represented the unwashed masses. And both of them promised to shake things up. For better or worse, they promised real change.

That's the last thing the DC cocktail party crowd wants!

The Biggest "Marks" Are in Politics

Politics has been this way forever. Most voters aren't stupid. They know it's all a show and they can see through it. It's simply what they have come to expect. That's why folks so often hold their nose and vote for the lesser of two evils.

The political class is a different story. Many of them actually believe that the mumbo jumbo they are peddling is real. Of course, they have to believe it—their livelihoods depend on it.

But here's the worst part: Most of them think they are smarter than we are. They believe they know what's good for us better than we know ourselves.

In wrestling, fans used to be derogatorily called "marks." "Mark" now refers to people who should know better but think it's real. Or someone who believes his own hype. For instance, when a wrestler's head gets too big, we'll say "he's a mark for himself."

The biggest marks aren't in wrestling, though. They are in politics.

Sadly, entire industries have now grown up around this perverted form of entertainment.

Cable TV, magazines, newspapers, digital marketing, and other forms of communication rely on politics for content. Everywhere we look, government is the story. You can't escape it. A few years ago, I was at a gym doing cardio. ESPN was covering congressional hearings about baseball, and it was on every TV.

Talk about spoiling a workout!

Politicians put on expensive suits and go on TV to tell us we must sacrifice our sons and daughters in wars in places we can't pronounce. They tell us we must sacrifice our liberties for the sake of security. They tell us we don't have the compassion to take care of one another so the government must do it. They tell us we must bail out billionaires. Worst of all, they tell us that we must hate and envy one another and that they are there to protect us from the other side.

Gee, I thought we were all Americans!

It's drama, pure and simple. Drama with an enormous price tag, both in dollars and freedom.

That's not to say there aren't some great people in politics. Folks who are real public servants and go about their work with little fanfare. People like Tennessee's current lieutenant governor, Randy McNally, who, early in his legislative career, put himself at great personal risk to root out corruption in the state capital.

Unfortunately, for every Randy McNally, there seem to be a dozen others in politics who are corrupt. For many politicians, it's not about public service. It's a game of ego and power. Don't expect them to give that up. We have to take their ball and tell them to go home.

The solution is not to just try to elect better people and hope they'll actually govern like they campaign. That hasn't worked.

The solution is to transform the system.

The Founding Fathers understood the dangers of unchecked political power. That's why the Constitution places strict limitations on the federal government.

Government simply should not have as much power over our lives as we have given it. Neither should politicians. If we want real change, at least at the national level, we must force the federal government back into its constitutional box.

Until we do that, the twisted reality show that passes for politics will continue to dominate our lives and our screens.

CHAPTER 12

I THINK I MIGHT BE A LIBERTARIAN

Who Knew?

I have been interested in politics since I was in high school. But I never felt like I aligned well with either side of the political spectrum. When trying to figure out what I believed, this was always a problem.

Like most people, I grew up thinking you had only two alternatives—the left or the right. I agreed with the right on some things, but disagreed on others. I agreed with the left on some things, but disagreed on others. I thought this made sense. Many Americans must feel this way, I believed.

No one politician or party is likely to have all the answers. Choosing a political party isn't like choosing a sports team, or at least shouldn't be. Picking your political ideology shouldn't be as clear-cut as deciding whether you should cheer for Hulk Hogan over the Iron Sheik, or for Steve Austin against Mr. McMahon.

It's easy to decide to become a fan of the Tennessee Titans, Hulkster, or Stone Cold.

But I find it harder to choose who to support in politics. There was always this pressure to choose a side. Was I left or right? Was I liberal or conservative? Was I a Democrat or a Republican?

I didn't know!

It All Began with Val Venis: What Do Libertarians Believe?

I felt politically homeless.

Until, one day, my friend and fellow WWE star Val Venis suggested I might be a libertarian. I wondered what that was. "You don't need to be calling me names!" I said to Val jokingly.

But I genuinely had no idea what that word even meant. I did some research and found the Libertarian Party, which was my first introduction to libertarianism. It seemed that this political label I had never heard of was home not only to some of the civil libertarian issues I cared about that had traditionally been on the left but also many of the economic freedom and limited-government ideas I subscribed to that were on the right.

I would soon learn these ideas weren't mutually exclusive. That, for all the things I agreed with Democrats and Republicans on, both parties also got some pretty big things wrong.

Left and right both make the big mistake of trying to compartmentalize human freedom. They make the false choice of saying, "Okay, I can have social liberty or I can have economic liberty," as if they were two separate things that can't coexist. The left tends to believe we have to give up our economic freedom in the name of social progress, and the right tends to believe social liberty can be bad, but not economic freedom. Both want to use the force of government to suppress certain freedoms while promoting others.

Libertarians believe that both social and economic freedom represent the same kind of liberty. They are not separate. If you don't have economic freedom, you also don't have personal liberty, and vice versa.

It's also not as simple as saying libertarians are "socially liberal" but "fiscally conservative." I'm a pretty conservative person on social issues. I just don't believe it is the government's role to mandate those behaviors. I'm conservative when it comes to economics, but the free-market ideas to which I subscribe are at the heart of what most political scientists would call "classical liberalism."

Confused yet? Blame that on our unimaginative, conventional politics.

But more people are seeing through the confusion. There's a reason more Americans today call themselves "independent" than ever before. People are fed up with politics as usual, and rightfully so.

Libertarianism Goes Beyond Left and Right

Me too. The fact that libertarianism turned the left-right dichotomy on its head was attractive to me. It was easy to reject the mainstream labels that never truly represented me anyway. Libertarianism encompassed my beliefs far more comprehensively than plain old left or right. I now had a political identity and philosophical framework for my beliefs.

I was excited to learn that there were others out there of like mind, including celebrities like Drew Carey, Vince Vaughn, Penn Jillette (of Penn & Teller), former MTV video jockey Kennedy (aka Lisa Kennedy Montgomery, who today has a great libertarian show on the Fox Business Network), and Clint Eastwood, among others.

Among the ranks of WWE, libertarians include not only Val Venis, but my friend Goldust.

Of course, I wanted to know more. When I get interested in something, I have to learn everything about it. That was the way I felt about my political and philosophical development.

Soon, I was reading economists, columnists, and free market thinkers like Milton Friedman, Ludwig von Mises, Frederic Bastiat, Judge Andrew Napolitano, Walter Williams. There were many more.

But the writer who probably had the most impact on me was Austrian economist Murray Rothbard. He was hard to argue with. Every objection from the left or right that anyone could possibly bring up, Rothbard would promptly destroy. For me, that was it. He was my guy.

Rothbard taught me about the "nonaggression principle," which is the defining basis for most libertarian thought. The nonaggression principle—or NAP—states that aggression (excluding the kind you see in pro wrestling!) is inherently wrong and can be used with justification only in defense of one's person or property. It coincides with the idea of self-ownership.

We are all individuals, first and foremost, with certain inalienable rights.

Once I had that philosophical grounding, I began to understand the basic truism that none of us has the right to impose our will on others through violence. And—most important—neither does the government.

Once you reach that conclusion, you start to become a libertarian.

Its principles extend to passing judgment on things others do that I might disagree with personally. I can't say that people should or should not do those things. They are their own people. I'm my own person.

As long as they're not hurting anyone with those choices, it's really up to them.

Ron Paul's "Revolution"

This was the message libertarian Ron Paul campaigned on when he ran for the Republican presidential nomination in 2008. That year, the Texas congressman became one of his party's most popular candidates, especially among young people.

Ron Paul did more to popularize libertarianism within our country's political system than anyone else has in my lifetime. For many, he became a household name.

Paul got one million votes in 2008 and went on to attract

double that number in 2012. Thousands of supporters—overwhelmingly young people—showed up at his rallies, whether they were held at conservative religious schools like Liberty University, in Lynchburg, Virginia, or liberal ones, like the University of California, Berkeley.

Paul's best allies in Congress were conservative Republicans, like my own former congressman, Jimmy Duncan of Knoxville, and liberal Democrats, like Dennis Kucinich of Ohio.

Ron Paul received praise from activist groups across the political spectrum, including from the right-leaning Freedom-Works and the left-leaning American Civil Liberties Union.

Remember what I said about libertarians turning the whole left-right thing on its head?

To the delight of many, Paul blasted through the left-right dichotomy. Many of his supporters were Republicans who had begun to think maybe their party was wrong about war and wrong about trying to tell others how to live their lives.

Others were Democrats who were becoming more conservative on economics.

Many were people who had never before cared about politics. "Dr. Paul cured my apathy" became a popular slogan.

I staunchly supported Ron Paul's bids for the GOP presidential nomination in 2008 and 2012. During that time, I saw many WWE and Kane fans become interested in Paul. In my own small way, I felt that my celebrity had helped further a cause that I was passionate about.

Despite having worked with celebrities for decades, I have been genuinely starstruck only once—the first time I shook Ron Paul's hand.

I probably felt the way many WWE fans do when they meet their favorite Superstar. They love WWE so much that, when they get to see wrestlers up close, they can be overwhelmed.

It's really a thrill, and I just wanted you to know that I totally get it.

As a staunch libertarian, my daily occupation at that time was still working to maintain my status as WWE Superstar, not politician or political philosopher. But here I was meeting the man who had done more for libertarianism in the United States than anyone. He was my hero. So, yes, it was a pretty big deal!

The Liberty Movement

It was thanks, in large part, to Ron Paul's popularity that his son Rand Paul won a seat in the U.S. Senate from Kentucky in 2010. Now that Ron Paul has retired from Congress, Rand has replaced him as the most high-profile libertarian in politics. I was proud that Rand endorsed my mayoral run in 2018, and I am honored he wrote a foreword for this book.

Because it was Republicans like him and his father who inspired me to run. Today, I'm a registered Republican and not part of the Libertarian Party. That was because developments occurred within the GOP after 2008 that let me know there was a place in the party for people like me.

Today in Congress, you have the House Liberty Caucus and the House Freedom Caucus, both of which are part of Ron Paul's legacy. Members of these caucuses include Rep.

Thomas Massie of Kentucky, one of the most libertarian members of Congress. My own former congressman, Jimmy Duncan, more often than not voted with libertarian Republicans, specifically on matters related to foreign policy. He and Ron Paul were two of the few Republicans who voted against the Iraq War.

The activist group Young Americans for Liberty—formerly "Students for Ron Paul"—is the largest center-right youth group in U.S. history. I have spoken at their conferences and other events as they continue to produce the next generation of libertarian stars. I run into lots of young wrestling fans at these conferences, too!

I'm proud to be part of this libertarian faction within the GOP. I'm also a proud Republican, but voters at home understood when they elected me to office that I was a different kind of Republican and would approach the daily business of running Knox County, Tennessee, in a different way.

I campaigned on those liberty-friendly themes and, thankfully, was elected. I was humbled on election night and remain so today.

I think that most of the people of Knox County and, indeed, most people across the country, whatever their political affiliation, share my fundamental belief that it should be up to each of us to decide how we want to pursue our own individual happiness.

I think libertarianism appeals to most people because that's how we lead our lives. We lead our lives in voluntary action with other folks, and we follow the nonaggression principle.

It's basically the Golden Rule! Who doesn't agree with the Golden Rule?

The thing about libertarianism is that it really helps each of us in our individual quests to achieve the American dream. It calls for everyone to be able to live their lives as they want, as long as doing so doesn't hurt anyone else.

Except in the wrestling ring! But, seriously, I can't help but think about the business I love in libertarian terms.

Speaking of which, did you know Vince McMahon's takeover of the pro-wrestling business in the 1980s can be explained by libertarian economics?

CHAPTER 13

HOW VINCE McMAHON TOOK OVER PRO WRESTLING IN THE '80s

As Explained by Austrian Economics

M any old-school wrestling fans still miss the days of the territories. I will always cherish the time I spent working for smaller wrestling companies like World Wrestling Council in Puerto Rico, USWA in Memphis, and Smoky Mountain Wrestling in Knoxville, but innovations in technology in the 1980s made it inevitable that the ways people were consuming entertainment—including professional wrestling—would change.

Vince McMahon has always stressed that he's in the entertainment business, and that the form of entertainment he promotes just happens to be pro wrestling.

Many don't understand how important it is to recognize this distinction.

Treating our business as entertainment first and foremost was always crucial to WWE's success. Vince McMahon—the greatest innovator professional wrestling has ever seen—had the wisdom to change with the times in ways other territory promoters either could not or would not, all to their ultimate detriment.

It has always been up to innovators to foresee and capitalize on changes in technology. Those who ignore the progress that free markets inevitably create always suffer for it.

This is not new.

During the twentieth century, owners of railroad companies thought they were in the railroad business; many didn't realize they were actually in the transportation business. Once the steam engine came along, demand for buggies and horsewhips tanked; once motor vehicles caught on, demand for trains plummeted.

And it didn't end there. Both trains and cars got some steep competition when man learned to take flight.

Similarly, in the 1980s, as satellite and cable technology exploded and prices dropped, the distribution of entertainment programming began to change. It was inevitable that the way people watched wrestling would change, too.

By recognizing this and acting on it, Vince prevailed over almost everyone else in the wrestling business, causing the industry to consolidate. Massive consolidations almost always occur in genuine free markets, and those consolidations are almost always challenged at a later date with major disruptions—which is what the thriving independent wrestling scene or even NXT have experienced during the last few years.

This is just a natural cycle inherent in free markets.

Why Vince Was Smarter Than the Music Industry

You have a massive consolidation because of technology, which in the '80s was the advent of cable television, something WWE led the way on in the wrestling industry. This consolidation was followed years later by a market disruption in the older system, which is what we see today with streaming services.

Many don't realize this, but Vince had been making plans for something like the WWE Network long before the technology was available for the model you see today. Bruce Prichard said he had a network in mind as far back as the early '80s, the time of the birth of Hulkamania. I had long heard he wanted to do something similar to the networks that carry Major League Baseball or the NFL.

Think about it. Why would Vince have bought WCW in 2001? I know he had various story line plans, but the organization was basically worthless to him long-term—except for their video library. As far as content goes, particularly for a future network, that video collection, going all the way back through the NWA and Jim Crockett Promotions, is priceless.

Streaming is not the only new(ish) technology disrupter today. So too is social media, and its ubiquity is forcing everyone in wrestling to adapt. Wrestlers can now build global fan bases in ways the old territory promoters could never have fathomed. The old territory promoters used to worry about people in other areas finding out about contradictory story lines, where a wrestler who was a face or a heel in one state might be the opposite in another.

For wrestlers today, thanks to social media, their territory extends around the world.

As the people who used to make their living selling buggy whips learned, it is not easy to avoid new technology. Those who try do so at their own peril. Vince was smart enough to avoid some of the bad decisions made by another major entertainment business that failed to embrace new technology—the music industry.

Remember the days of massive lawsuits by record companies over fans sharing MP3s? The record companies had a point in complaining that the new technology allowed their products to be pirated by consumers, who were listening to their products without paying for them. The bottom line: The record companies were losing big money.

But it was also simply a fact that digital downloads and music sharing were here to stay. There was no putting the genie back in the bottle.

Customers want what they want, and the market is going to do what it's going to do. The most connected politician or brilliant economist isn't going to change this powerful dynamic.

Instead of trying to capitalize on new technology as well as it could, the music industry instead tried to fight it, and to what end? The method of distributing music wasn't going to change. The market delivered what music fans demanded. It was inevitable, even as music business honchos resisted it to the very end.

To quote *Star Trek*, "Resistance is futile!"—when it comes to the market.

WWE has wisely taken a different approach with emerging social media. There was a time—before smartphones and Twitter—when the quickest way to get in trouble at a WWE show was to be seen with a camera.

Our product still is our intellectual property, and there are still restrictions on what fans can and cannot share from a WWE live event. But wise business executives still have to recognize when technology significantly changes their business. If they don't, they will always lose.

Can you imagine how ridiculous it would be today, in the age of smartphones, to try to ban the taking of photographs?? So many fans go to WWE shows for that very reason: to take photos of themselves with their friends, or even quick captures of their favorite Superstars.

Vince was smarter than the record industry. He embraced this technology.

Today, WWE encourages fans to share their photos on social media and even provides hashtags to help promote their posts as widely as possible. WWE has even aired matches on Facebook Watch and promotes these online events during their television broadcasts. All WWE Superstars and personalities have their own Twitter and Instagram accounts, where they embrace and interact with fans in ways that have never been seen in the wrestling business.

Some of them even have story lines their fans enjoy that are separate from what you see on WWE television and the WWE Network. A number of years ago, Zack Ryder might have been one of the first Superstars to truly understand how much performers could use a platform like YouTube to promote themselves. Zack was underutilized in WWE to the point where he feared for his livelihood. Then he created *Z! True Long Island Story*, his own YouTube show, which he used to showcase his personality and revamp his character. Seemingly overnight, WWE crowds began chanting, "We want Ryder!" That was in 2011. To this day, Zack is still in WWE and has built a fine career for himself.

There's so much going on, fans couldn't take in all the social media activity by their favorite Superstars even if they wanted to—though many try! You might have even bought this book because of a tweet or Facebook recommendation.

All of this promotion helps WWE and sports entertainment overall. It's part of the ongoing global revolution in how we consume wrestling.

What Is Austrian Economics?

Like cable before it, the internet has disrupted and decentralized the wrestling market. This is all thanks to advances in technology, for which we can credit innovation. And we can credit competition and capitalism for the innovation that we see everywhere in this country.

The market satisfies everyone's needs at an organically set

price. It's a wonderful thing—people having the freedom to make their own decisions about what to do with their own money.

What a time to be alive! What a time to be a wrestling fan!

Again, as technology has changed, so has entertainment and, thus, so has pro wrestling.

This may seem predictable in hindsight, but in real time, how human beings choose to spend their money and what kind of innovation will arise from trying to serve that market is not something even the smartest economist in the world can necessarily foresee.

These types of revolutionary market changes—including how pro wrestling has evolved over the last half century—can be best understood through something called Austrian economics.

Austrian economics? you may ask. What the heck is that? Is that about what some post–World War II foreign heel wrestler got paid back in the 1950s?

Maybe a tag team? *"And in this corner, hailing from Vienna, weighing in at a combined weight of 535 pounds, The Austrians!"*

Not quite. But there was a time when I would have asked the same questions.

Austrian economics is a school of thought to which many libertarian and free-market thinkers like me subscribe. We believe that the market works best when talented and industrious individuals are allowed to conduct their business with limited government interference.

When entrepreneurs are allowed to pursue profit, mostly

unfettered, society benefits as a whole. Innovation occurs. Jobs are created. There will always be "booms" and "busts" in any economy—but those high points can be greater and low points less damaging to the degree that government stays out of the way, something it rarely does.

Austrian-American Ludwig von Mises—a Jewish economist who fled the Nazis in 1940, and who is considered one of the greatest minds of the Austrian school—had one major rule when it came to those who studied economics:

The first job of an economist is to tell governments what they cannot do.

First and foremost? Government cannot create wealth. Only private individuals within the free market can do that. The best that government can do, for the most part, is to stay out of the way.

Think about it: There's no way government could have created WWE—but Vince McMahon could.

The beauty of Austrian economics is that it studies how things work in the real world. Economics is not a predictive science, despite what many "experts" presume. You can't say, *"If we do this, this is what's gonna happen."*

Life doesn't work that way. And that's not how human beings interact with money.

A lot of the old wrestling-territory promoters who made a lot of money for many years thought that if they kept doing business the same way, they would continue to be successful. They had little imagination or vision beyond what was right in front of them. If their money had always flowed in a certain way, it stood to reason that it always would.

But it didn't turn out that way.

At one time, some forty wrestling territories existed in the United States, Canada, and Mexico. They were all generally successful because the individual promoters who ran them produced the only wrestling the fans in each locale knew. They were the only game in town, literally.

At that time, there was little to no competition in pro wrestling among the many various brands. When you include the fact that few markets had more than three television stations, the promoters had all the advantages. No one could touch them.

Each territory kept out of the other territories' business. They did not compete, in the same way that the mob didn't compete. Each family had its own exclusive areas of operation, just as street gangs have their own "turf."

In wrestling, each territory had its own stars, story lines, and brands: the American Wrestling Association (AWA) in Minneapolis; World Class Championship Wrestling (WCCW) in Dallas; Stu Hart's Stampede Wrestling in Calgary; Bill Watts's Mid-South Wrestling in Oklahoma; Jim Crockett's Mid-Atlantic Championship Wrestling in Charlotte; Mike Graham's Florida Championship Wrestling; Jerry Lawler's Memphis Wrestling. There were far too many to list them all here.

Many wrestling fans, myself included, have fond memories of the old territories. It's the wrestling I grew up on.

Some of the biggest stars in the history of professional wrestling and WWE started out in these territories—Hulk Hogan, Ric Flair, Roddy Piper, Sting, Steve Austin—you name it.

But they all became even bigger stars after cable came along. More than a few didn't become globally known megastars until they worked for WWE.

Just ask Hulk Hogan.

I'm proud to have witnessed firsthand at least the tail end of those old days of wrestling early in my career. In fact, my time in Smoky Mountain Wrestling coincided with Jim Cornette's attempt to keep the spirit of the territories alive—something, ironically, WWE had a hand in helping support for a time (if you will recall, my first match against Undertaker wasn't even in WWE).

Still, those many territories did not compete with each other. There wasn't really a free market among the different organizations. It was understood by all involved that they stayed within their own areas. The established promotions even had a name for upstarts who tried to encroach on their space—"outlaw promotions."

Competition was simply a big no-no in the old days of wrestling.

Cable and Pay-per-View Changed the Wrestling Economy

As their old business model was perishing, many of those territory promoters could have benefitted from understanding Austrian economics, which is more of a descriptive science— in other words, it describes what's going on.

During the 1980s, the old promoters had no idea what was going on.

But Vince did. He saw that cable television was going on.

He saw that closed-circuit television extravaganzas and, later, pay-per-view was going on.

Overall, he saw that technological progress in entertainment was going on.

Vince's early read of the market changes led him to create events like *WrestleMania* and WWE wrestling on the USA Network. (It should be noted that Jim Crockett Promotions' *Starrcade* events, the brainchild of Dusty Rhodes, the head of creative for Crockett, preceded *WrestleMania* in closed-circuit events, and NWA Wrestling on Ted Turner's Superstation got under way before Vince set up his USA deal for WWE. However, virtually all parties involved today will tell you that no one had the vision and business wherewithal that Vince did in predicting how these technological advancements would change wrestling's future.)

By the early 1980s, Vince knew that the idea of regional promotions using local one-hour TV wrestling shows to get people to the school gymnasium or county hall for wrestling every Tuesday night wasn't going to last much longer.

It would be as if the producers of *Gunsmoke*, the popular radio program of the 1950s, never made the jump to television. Regional promoters of the 1980s needed to adapt in the same fashion, but the majority either didn't realize it or were too set in their ways.

It was one of those old territorial promotions—the New York–based company owned by Vince McMahon Sr.—that would eventually become the dominant brand in wrestling: WWE. It happened because the younger McMahon went on to buy the company from his father and begin to compete.

For the first time in decades, the wrestling business became competitive.

And no one knew what to do.

"No one had any idea cable TV was coming out," Pat Patterson—WWE legend, Vince's closest friend of many years, and my friend—told *Business Insider* in 2016. "They see that show in LA, they see that show in St. Louis, they see that show in Minneapolis...

" 'Wow, what is that kid Vince McMahon doing? He's ruining us!' " Patterson said. "And I'm going to tell you something... they hated him!"

But many wrestlers in the promotions loved what Vince was doing. Those talented enough began to leave the territories for greater fame and more money working with Vince.

Unlike the promoters, wrestlers were comfortable with competition. After all, they were used to competing with each other within those territories. They knew what it meant to strive to be better than the other guys. Each wanted their spot within their respective companies, particularly the top spot. Most had traveled among all the different territories throughout their careers.

Yes, the wrestlers, if not the promoters, knew exactly what competition was all about. They recognized Vince's move to compete in a free market as something that could help them— while the promoters doubled down on their old ways and simply griped about what WWE was doing to the industry.

The old territories went out of business because they stopped creating new stars when they couldn't move on from their outdated methods of promoting pro wrestling. They refused to change with the times. They did it to themselves.

Vince created competition in their business for the first time, and they didn't like it.

That's what happens when you ignore the free market.

Monday Night War

Of course, Vince would eventually see his stiffest competition to date from Ted Turner beginning in 1988, when Turner bought Jim Crockett Promotions and renamed it World Championship Wrestling, or WCW.

Turner had his own cable company. That would prove to be the common denominator for success in national wrestling from the 1980s into the '90s, when the industry went through its second boom period of the modern era.

But again, it was the advent of cable TV itself that had changed the wrestling game, something Vince predicted when few others did (some of the last wrestling territories standing like the AWA and WCCW would eventually reach deals with ESPN for national cable exposure, but these organizations didn't last long before their demise. It would end up being too little, too late).

Every wrestling fan also knows that billionaire Ted Turner's resources and the fact that he owned a cable company gave WWE the biggest run for its money in the '90s during the Monday Night War—one of the most exciting times in the history of pro wrestling. WWE's Attitude Era, of which I was a major part, developed in response to WCW creating a more popular product—for a time.

And why? Because of competition.

Everyone benefits when there is a true free market and different companies are competing for consumer dollars. This was true when Vince upended the old territory system by competing with the old promoters. It was true when Eric Bischoff came up with the New World Order idea in 1996 in Turner's WCW to challenge WWE head-on, beating Vince in the TV ratings for eighty-three weeks in a row. It's still true today, with so many independent wrestling companies flourishing as alternatives to WWE.

The transformations undergone by the wrestling business reflect the impact of the laissez-faire Austrian economics that I support.

As famed Anglo-Austrian economist F. A. Hayek—a favorite of former U.S. president Ronald Reagan—once said, "The curious task of economics is to demonstrate to men how little they really know about what they imagine they can design."

Vince didn't create wrestling. He didn't create cable. He didn't create the internet.

But he knew how to expand wrestling, to make it better and to grow the business beyond anyone's wildest dreams. He knew how to do this based on what was occurring naturally in the free market.

You Don't Have to Be an Expert to Understand Economics

"Keynesian economics"—the prevailing economic model among mainstream economists—does not reflect how things work in the real world. It's why so many economists consistently get things wrong.

Unlike Keynesians, Austrian economists believe the economy runs itself, and all that we're trying to do is understand how the economy really works.

Once you start reading about Austrian economics, this starts to make sense. Once you start to understand that economics is not about numbers, but about people—about human action—everything becomes clear.

I am not an economist. You shouldn't take what I say at face value. However, you also shouldn't just automatically believe those writing about this stuff just because they have a PhD in economics.

For example, virtually all major economists failed to see the 2007–2008 financial crisis coming with the exception of one group—members of the Austrian school. People in politics like Ron Paul, who also subscribes to Austrian economics, had been predicting a collapse for years. These Austrian observers knew that too many people with poor credit histories were buying too many homes for the market to be sustainable. Today, everyone agrees that that was how the housing market imploded more than a decade ago.

But all the "experts" at the time predicted that the economy would be just fine—right until the bottom fell out.

I never took a course in economics in college because I'm not very interested in math. My sister is a mathematician—a rocket scientist who used to work for NASA. She, not I, inherited the math gene in my family.

But I became attracted to Austrian economics the moment

I realized that everything that I had been taught about economics in school, and everything I had read about economics in mainstream publications, was wrong.

If economics is a hard science, most economists should agree—and yet few do. Put a dozen of them in a room and you'll get a dozen different opinions. And then, whatever unfolds with the economy, nine out of ten of them are usually wrong.

They are not stupid. In fact, they're a lot smarter than I am, especially if they have PhDs in economics. But they're just studying numbers and algebraic formulas. They're developing computer models.

That's not the way the real world works. That's not how human beings function and interact. No one can predict with scientific certainty how humans will act, react, or interact.

For all his genius, even Vince McMahon did not predict how big Hulkamania would get in the 1980s. He certainly didn't predict that Turner's WCW would almost drive WWE out of business a decade later. All of this surprised him more than anyone.

But he did see plenty of developments on the horizon that virtually no other promoter saw. He bought as many of the territories that were willing to sell to him as possible, and put the rest out of business—not because he was a mean guy, but because in the wrestling business, like any other, you either change with the times or get left behind.

"In the old days, there were wrestling fiefdoms all over the country, each with its own little lord in charge," Vince told *Sports Illustrated* in 1991. "There were maybe 30 of these tiny kingdoms in the U.S., and if I hadn't bought out my dad, there would still be 30 of them, fragmented and struggling."

Exactly. Despite what some of the old territory promoters might believe, that old business model would have struggled to survive past the '80s (and the few that did survive that long all struggled). It's almost impossible to imagine most of them thriving in the same form today. (Independent wrestling is thriving, and in some ways is similar to the old territories, but the alternatives to WWE that are successful today are based on an entirely different business model than the territories.)

It's really hard to imagine what the professional wrestling business would look like today if not for Vince McMahon and WWE. If not Vince, someone else would have capitalized on the cable revolution of the '80s. The free market would have seen to that. It was inevitable that some entrepreneur would eventually capitalize on closed-circuit and pay-per-view television—and technically, it was the always brilliant Dusty Rhodes who did it first with *Starrcade*—yet it was Vince who perfected it beyond what anyone else in the business could have ever envisioned.

It was Vince who did all these things, and it was Vince who did them best. But perhaps most important, it was Vince who did them first.

Because he always recognized that he was in the entertainment business.

CHAPTER 14

DONALD TRUMP, WWE HALL OF FAMER

And President of the United States

When I decided to run for mayor, I met with Vince to let him know my plans. He was completely supportive, as I expected him to be. He likes when his stars achieve great things outside the business, and he has always been invested in our success as human beings.

Our discussion that day, naturally, turned to politics. Vince has known and worked with Donald Trump for a long time. Vince told me Donald always tells it like it is, or at least as he sees it, no matter what.

It was surreal to hear Vince talking about "Donald" like he's just some guy. He's the president of the United States! Even as long as I've known and worked for Vince, I couldn't get it out of my head that I was sitting there talking to someone who knows the president.

Trump has been involved with WWE for decades, including *WrestleMania IV* in 1988 and *WrestleMania V* in 1989, both of which were held at Trump Plaza in Atlantic City, New Jersey.

The only direct contact I had with Trump during my time in WWE occurred in 2007 during the weeks leading up to *WrestleMania 23*, where Trump faced off against Vince in a "Battle of the Billionaires" head-shaving match. Bobby Lashley fought for Trump while Umaga was in Vince's corner. Steve Austin was the guest referee.

If you don't know who won, you must have been living under a rock since 2016, because I don't know how many times we've seen replays of Trump shaving Vince's head on every network and cable news outlet since he announced he was running for president. During their rivalry, Vince was always bragging about how big his "grapefruits" were.

Trump told Vince one night, "Your grapefruits are no match for my Trump Towers."

That wasn't too far off from some of President Trump's tweets!

Trump was always friendly and gracious to everyone backstage, including me. A friend of mine who doesn't really pay close attention to politics, a popular WWE star, told me he voted for Trump because he was a business guy, but also because of how nice the future president treated him backstage.

Like Him or Not, Trump Upset the Establishment

After I was elected mayor, I was invited to the White House to watch President Trump sign legislation intended to address the opioid crisis, an ongoing tragedy that has affected the entire country, and certainly Knox County.

The signing happened right after threatening packages had been sent to a number of prominent Democrats. When the president spoke to the news media that day, it was the first thing he was asked about. Of course, he said it was terrible and condemned all political violence.

Yet, later that day and into the evening, some media personalities tried to say the president had ignored these domestic acts of terrorism and walked out on reporters after he was asked about them. That was not what happened at all. I know because I was standing right there.

It was yet another example of the habitual duplicity of the media that makes so many Americans suspicious of and negative toward them. People say Trump is driving the divisiveness in our country. He isn't. He's a product of it. Both parties have been serving up plenty of divisiveness since long before Trump came onto the political scene.

President Trump did not invent the discord that plagues our politics, but he did capitalize on it. Most politicians do. Many of his critics seem to be angry that Trump's been far more successful at it than most.

The president, to his credit, has tried some things that

most conventional politicians would never have tried. Trump captured a portion of the Democrats' base by appealing to their traditional voters, especially in the Rust Belt. While his opponent ignored certain cities and states that had been traditional Democratic strongholds, Trump went there and campaigned.

Another attribute of the president is that, despite his wealth and success, he's not an elitist. Regular Americans can relate to him. This is something many in the political class can't understand. It drives them bonkers.

Many Americans see the president as caring about their problems when no one else in Washington does. So many Democrats, left-leaning members of the news media, and entertainment figures, dripping with smug elitism, have a hard time understanding Trump's appeal. Since they can't understand it, they dismiss it.

Of course, in the process, they have alienated middle America and the rest of the "fly-over country." Here's a bit of advice for leftist elitists: Just because someone disagrees with you doesn't mean they're stupid.

There are many things I like about Donald Trump and some things I don't, but one thing is certain: More than any other president in my lifetime, he has exposed the massive divide—politically, culturally, maybe even emotionally—between the political class and the average person.

This divide was on full display the night I watched the 2016 presidential election from a place that gave me a unique perspective: the United Kingdom.

Watching the 2016 Election Results in the UK

WWE was on tour in the UK, and as I watched things unfold that night—five hours ahead of Eastern Standard Time in the United States—part of my brain was thinking, "There's no way Trump can win." Virtually no one—no journalist, pundit, or pollster—began election night predicting that Trump would beat Hillary Clinton.

Then he did. I remember FiveThirtyEight's Nate Silver, one of the best political analysts, was one of the few who predicted a strong finish by Trump—and even his numbers slightly favored Clinton!

I really should have trusted my own observations more than what everyone was saying on television. As I've noted, WWE performers travel a lot, and I had been through about a half-dozen presidential elections during my time with the company. Based on my U.S. travel in 2015 and 2016 and on the lack of campaign signs I saw, the presidential race seemed to me to be among the least exciting races I had seen.

But the few signs I did see were almost *all* Trump signs. I saw at least ten times more signs for Donald Trump than I saw signs for Hillary Clinton—everywhere I went. Of course, Clinton signs outnumbered Trump signs in urban areas, but there were far more Trump signs overall in my travels.

The media got it so wrong because, as members of the political class, they are disconnected from the public. Even most who voted for Clinton weren't excited enough about her to put out a yard sign.

I watched the election play out on a television in my Glasgow, Scotland, hotel room. Because of the time difference, it was 3 or 4 a.m. before I had a pretty good idea of who would win.

I got my first inkling when media outlets began focusing on Pennsylvania, with the talking heads saying Clinton didn't have enough numbers in that state to win. Then they began saying the same thing about Michigan. Outgoing president Barack Obama had won both states in 2008 and 2012. They were key states.

That was when I knew Trump was about to become our next president. I couldn't go to sleep. I couldn't stop watching TV. Reporters were still breaking down individual districts in states at 5 a.m. in the UK. When they finally called it for Trump, obviously, many in the United States, especially members of the news media, were shocked.

But that was nothing compared to the UK coverage.

The foreign press totally freaked out. Full meltdown. They were more unprepared for a Trump victory than the American media was. Their coverage of the U.S. election results was more like a response to a terrorist attack.

Obviously, given America's standing in the world, U.S. politics and elections are always going to reverberate globally. But I had never seen anything like this.

I remember one pundit recalling that Trump had said perhaps the United States should pull out of NATO. He wondered who was going to defend Europe.

I was thinking, "How about Europe?" Seemed simple enough to me.

I thought, "Well, the U.S. is going to have to live with it, I guess the UK will, too." Then, finally, I went to bed.

In one night, Donald Trump had upended the entire status quo on a global scale. When we look around the planet, we can see that there really is an elitism, what many call "globalism," that binds the political class. Meanwhile, much like William Graham Sumner's "forgotten man," many people feel as if no cares about them. Like him or not, Trump spoke to them. I believe that a major reason Trump won was that many voters were simply tired of the same old politicians.

If any other Republican had won the 2016 election—with the exception of libertarian Republican Rand Paul—the elites would not have freaked out the way they did with Trump. They would not have cared. The angst wouldn't have been there.

That's because the imminent disruption to the status quo wouldn't have been hanging over their heads.

While Trump's win was a strike against elitism, or "globalism," that doesn't mean globalism is uniformly a bad thing. Globalism through genuine free trade is actually a good thing, for the United States and the rest of the world.

On the surface, I don't like Trump's tariffs. But I think I understand what he's doing. He's trying to create a stronger negotiating position. The president has even said via Twitter that if every other country would drop their tariffs, we could drop ours, too. Then everyone could have real free trade.

As a businessman, I believe Trump is trying to push things as far as he can with other countries to get the best deal that he can. As president, that's his job. He's not enacting tariffs and other policies willy-nilly. Trump is applying common business practices to economics, even global economics.

Tariffs are taxes. What's amazing to me is that so many who criticize Trump's tariffs—which are essentially international taxes—always want to jack up taxes astronomically in the United States. They pretend to hate taxes on other countries, but have no problem with taking every last cent from your pocket!

Democrats may not admit it, but President Trump has done more with criminal-justice reform than any president in my lifetime, giving nonviolent offenders who have endured ridiculously long sentences a second chance. His deregulation directives have helped the economy, as did his tax cut. And he has repeatedly voiced his intention to end America's longest war in Afghanistan, something long overdue. It's time to bring our brave soldiers home.

I really loved it when Trump appointed Linda McMahon as head of the Small Business Administration! If there was ever a person born for that role, it's Linda.

If Trump Can Win, Why Not Kane?

I wish we could get to a point in our politics where we begin judging leaders by who they are and how they lead, and not on whether they have an "R" or "D" by their name. So many people hate Donald Trump just because he's a Republican. That doesn't do anyone any good.

The best thing about Trump's victory is that it sent a

message to the political establishment. Someone needed to rattle their cage, and he did.

That last part is so important for me personally. Donald Trump was never supposed to win.

When he won, I knew I could, too.

Trump's election showed there was massive unrest among voters across the nation. I laughed when so many observers were surprised that antiestablishment candidates were winning state and local races too, in *both parties*.

It's a national phenomenon at all levels of politics and it will continue. People want something new.

Trump is not a politician. Neither am I. That gives me an incredible amount of freedom to do the right thing. If I do the right thing and lose the next election because of it, I won't be bothered at all. I have many other things that I could do. While most politicians say that, in my case it's true. My livelihood is not dependent on my staying in office. The same is true for Trump.

I tell myself every day that I don't need this job. That keeps me objective. And that objectivity is important if I'm going to do a good job for the people of Knox County.

While a trash-talking, reality TV star convinced me that if he could become president, Kane could become mayor, there's still one big thing Donald Trump has accomplished that I haven't: becoming a member of the WWE Hall of Fame.

Maybe one day. A boy can dream!

CHAPTER 15

AMERICA REALLY IS THE GREATEST COUNTRY IN THE WORLD

As I look back over my life, one thing is apparent: There is no way it should have turned out like this. After all, I grew up on a small farm in the middle of nowhere. I failed at everything I tried before I finally made it. I'm not that smart or talented or exceptionally gifted.

In many ways, it feels like I've won the lottery. But has it all been blind luck?

The answer, I think, is yes and no.

No, because I put in the work. I was determined and I persevered. I refused to stop until I had achieved my goal. Hard work and determination are integral ingredients in anyone's success.

But there is something else you must have as well. And that's where luck kicks in.

I had opportunity.

Throughout my entire life, I've had tremendous opportunities to utilize my talents, my gifts, and my skills. Without those opportunities, all those gifts would have gone unused, wasted. The same is true for all of us.

But it's not like opportunity is the result of blind luck. I created some of those opportunities through my willingness to work, to take risks, and to step outside of my comfort zone.

America Is Great Thanks to the Free Market

I'm lucky because I live in a country where such opportunities become available. I live in the United States of America. There is nothing special about America itself, however. What is special is our free-market economy. Without that, opportunities would be few and far between and directly tied to a person's political connections.

That's not to say America is perfect. Tragically, our economy has veered increasingly toward state capitalism, also called crony capitalism and corporatism. This is what happens when government rigs the system to favor certain entities. It's one thing for people to sink or swim in a true free market. It's quite another for the government to shield them unfairly or to play favorites, which is what we see so often today.

Big corporations and big money exercise way too much control over policy and regulations. We saw great examples of this during the Great Recession of 2007–2008, when Congress bailed out billionaires in the banking sector and propped up a failing General Motors.

Nevertheless, our free-market legacy is still strong and productive. The American Dream is still alive.

You see, the American Dream is not about things, as it has often been perversely portrayed. It's not about stuff. It's about the freedom to create the life you want to live; to use your talents and gifts in the pursuit of happiness.

A few years ago, I took a cab to Reagan National Airport outside Washington. The driver told me he was from Africa and had recently come to the United States.

"What are you doing here, so far from home?" I asked.

"Because this *is America*!" he replied. He then explained that he had left his home and his family to come here...to drive a cab! But driving a cab was simply his doorway in. In his words, anyone can make it in America.

In his home country, there were no opportunities for socioeconomic advancement, he said. Wherever a person was born on the social-status ladder was likely where that person would die.

Not so in America. He said he was planning to save some of the money he made as a cabbie and use those savings to buy his own taxi, start his own business, or go to school. At home, such opportunities wouldn't exist, he added.

We have a lot of shortcomings here in America. We have flaws. We have warts. It is important to be introspective, to be self-critical. But it is also important to be honest about what the real problems are.

Those problems are not inherent in the American Dream

itself. Far from it. They exist because the American Dream has been denied to certain groups because of things like institutional racism, generational dependency on government programs, lack of socioeconomic advancement, and creeping crony capitalism.

All these things represent the antithesis of what America stands for. But we are constantly inundated with cries to destroy what makes our country great in a misguided attempt to fix what's wrong with it.

Needless to say, this would be a huge mistake.

When addressing our problems, we often see a knee-jerk reaction, one that blames capitalism and the free market and calls for more government regulation and intervention, moves that would undermine our freedom to choose and act.

While many push for government solutions, they rarely ask the important question: Why?

Government Is the Problem

What causes many of our problems? We stop at the superficial. We see the symptoms and turn to Dr. Big Government to fix them without even asking for a diagnosis. If the doctor were to give that diagnosis, they would be forced to say that they are the disease.

Often, the government tries to fix things that aren't really broken, and ends up making matters worse. Instead of acknowledging what they've done, politicians write more laws to try to mitigate the damage. Of course, this makes things worse still, so we get another round of laws. And the cycle continues.

For example, take health care. Before World War II, people paid for doctors' visits and many procedures out of pocket. Health insurance was only for catastrophic events. It was like car insurance. You pay for routine maintenance out of pocket and have insurance for wrecks and other catastrophes.

That changed during WWII, when the government started getting involved. Because of President Franklin Delano Roosevelt's wage and price controls, companies could no longer compete for employees by offering higher wages, so they began to offer and sponsor group health insurance to workers. As a result, third-party payers—insurance companies— replaced the out-of-pocket system. With consumers no longer paying the majority of the bills directly, there was no incentive for them to control their spending and costs. This sowed the seeds for higher health care costs.

From there, we saw the introduction of programs like Medicare and Medicaid. Both of these programs ended up being massively more expensive than originally projected. To cope with problems like rising costs and limited access—problems they had caused—Congress passed the Health Maintenance Organization (HMO) Act of 1973.

Again, this only made things worse. Not only did HMOs fail to contain costs, they limited consumer choice and, in some cases, denied care altogether. Ironically, years later, it became vogue for Congress to criticize HMOs, organizations that Congress itself played a major role in creating.

As the years passed, government continued to insinuate itself more deeply into health care and prices continued to rise. By 2010, the year Congress passed the Affordable Care

Act (ACA)—Obamacare—the government controlled 44 percent of the money spent on health care in the United States. Throw in a boatload of regulations and mandates, and our free market in medicine doesn't look so free.

The funny thing is that despite all the government spending, regulations, and interventions, few people actually looked at the evidence and asked the important question: Is government the problem, not the solution?

Instead, the "free market" took the blame. So along comes the ACA, a panacea to fix something that government broke to begin with. The promise was a more affordable and accessible health care system.

That hasn't exactly turned out as advertised, to say the least. Health insurance is more expensive than ever. The insurance market has consolidated—not as a result of market forces in which the best companies rise to the top through the competitive process, but because government policies nearly always benefit large, established players, stifling competition and, thus, consumer choice; and federal spending continues to increase to support the program. Meanwhile, sky-high deductibles mean that many low-income workers who gained coverage under the ACA are still, for all practical purposes, uninsured. Proponents of the ACA point to its mandate requiring insurers to cover people with preexisting conditions as proof of increased accessibility to health insurance. What they ignore is the increased cost of health insurance for all of us, especially the 28 million Americans who remain without health insurance, in many cases because they can't afford it.

Compare how we have handled health care to the way

we've handled the electronics industry. While the cost of health care keeps going up, the cost of cell phones, computers, TVs, and other devices keeps dropping, even as the quality improves exponentially. Granted, the electronics industry is still relatively new and being driven by massive innovation, but it is subject to much less regulation than health care.

Could you imagine what the cell phone industry would look like if the government controlled it in the same manner that it controls health care? Actually, we don't have to look that far back. Thanks to government regulations restricting competition, AT&T enjoyed a monopoly on telephone service in the United States for decades. The result was passable service and reasonable pricing.

But when the federal government ordered the breakup of the monopoly that was the Bell Telephone Company in 1982 (known to many as "Ma Bell"), introducing competition into the system, innovation took off. Fewer than forty years later, telecommunications are light-years ahead of where they had been.

While Ma Bell's monopoly might have seemed reasonable, perhaps even necessary during its time, it inhibited innovation and we were stuck with the same technologies for seventy years. In fact, Ma Bell, and more so the Federal Communications Commission (FCC), might have delayed the development of cell phones for decades.

Believe it or not, the cell phone concept was first introduced to the public in 1945! Being a monopoly, Ma Bell had little incentive to develop this promising idea. Meanwhile, the FCC refused to issue licenses and allocate space on the radio spectrum for cellular phone usage for decades.

After all that, the first commercial cell phone was finally introduced in 1983. Adjusted for inflation, DynaTac's iconic "Brick" was a steal at $8,806!

The free market has a track record of producing results: innovation, lower prices, response to consumer demand. When we look at living standards around the world, this is the best time in human history to be alive, at least from a materialistic perspective. Even issues like pollution are getting better. It turns out that, as a society becomes more affluent, people can stop worrying about things like food and shelter, and concentrate instead on issues like the environment.

If Government Ran WWE

Can you imagine if we took a socialist approach to sports entertainment? An America and world where free-market competition isn't allowed—and pro wrestling is instead controlled by the government? As many products and services are in oppressive regimes?

Think of the worst wrestling you can imagine. Maybe WCW just before it was about to go under and had been reduced to "Viagra on a Pole" matches, but even a hundred times worse than that! That's exactly what you would get with government-sponsored wrestling. Bureaucrats just doling out whatever fodder they were obligated to dole out, with no market demand by consumers to get the best possible products delivered to them.

Do you like or hate John Cena? Bureaucrats wouldn't care either way. You want more Charlotte Flair and Becky Lynch?

Government paper pushers wouldn't care less. You want to see the Brothers of Destruction one last time? Government wouldn't care what you want. They'd have no incentive to.

Because there's no competition, no innovation, and no pressure to meet market demand.

No good.

The free market is the greatest wealth-producing machine the world has ever known. In no place is this more evident than in America. If you figure out a way to take advantage of your God-given gifts and talents, if you work hard, and if you persist and never give up, there is no telling what you can do.

I've seen it happen in my own life. We all know stories of Americans who came from the most humble of beginnings to succeed on an epic scale. Almost every day, I meet folks who have lived stories of success that are possible only here, in a place where they had the freedom to use their gifts and take advantage of opportunities to realize their full potential.

Despite all of this, the American Dream is under attack. How can that be?

It's because, despite overwhelming evidence to the contrary, socialism's promises of government-generated wealth and comfort have made a resurgence.

Of course, those pushing this line insist that this time it's different. This time, socialism will be implemented successfully. You see, it's not the concept or system that's the problem, they contend. It's just that the people running the system have not gotten it right yet.

It always helps when you slap a different name on it, too.

This time it's "democratic socialism." Things always sound better when you incorporate the term "democratic."

In pro wrestling, we call it "repackaging" when someone undergoes a character change. The difference here is that nothing has changed about the socialist paradigm.

It reminds me of the Who song "Won't Get Fooled Again": "Meet the new boss. Same as the old boss." No matter the packaging, the Boss in socialism is always Big Government, and its arrival is always accompanied by the loss of individual liberty.

Socialism Is the Antithesis of Freedom

The promise of socialism is that government will take care of you. You'll always be guaranteed a place to live, food to eat, and the other necessities of life. The one thing missing is freedom.

As President Dwight Eisenhower once observed, "If you want total security, go to prison. There, you're fed, clothed, given medical care and so on. The only thing lacking…is freedom."

What socialism really promises is a comfortable box: one that you'll spend your life in. You'll be protected, you'll have your basic needs met, but you can never break out. You won't be allowed to fail, which means you'll never experience what you are truly capable of.

Most of us who seek to reach the heights for which we are destined will fail along the way. Time and time again. I've done it in my own life. Failing is actually an integral part of achieving success.

What would have happened if I merely existed in that comfortable box? I would never have felt the need to move forward or push myself in any way. It would have been easy to quit.

The hidden truth of the socialist promise is that it guarantees mediocrity. You aren't on this earth to be mediocre. You are here to be great. You can only be great if you are allowed to seize your destiny . . . and have the freedom to fail along the way.

The reality of socialism is completely different. Socialism inevitably results in poverty, misery, and death. Socialists will point to examples of success without acknowledging that it is the market that props up socialist programs. As government takes over more and more of an economy, things get worse and worse.

The question socialists never answer honestly is, "Who pays for it?"

The usual answer, "Oh, we'll just tax the rich," is disingenuous. Everyone pays. And they all pay a lot. Socialists promise a free lunch. But that lunch comes at a horrible cost, both to our finances and to our freedoms.

America is not just a place. It's an ideal. An ideal that promises that everyone is free to pursue their dreams. Free to utilize their gifts, talents, and work. And free to keep the fruits of their labor and to create the life of their dreams.

It would be a shame if that ideal were to die.

Despite its flaws, America is still a beacon of freedom and liberty. The world would be a darker place without it.

CHAPTER 16

———

MAYOR KANE

O n the night of my Republican primary election for mayor, I
was on the phone with my campaign manager, Bryan Hair.
He said we were down by five hundred votes after early voting.

This was not the news I wanted to hear.

It was unquestionably the most stressful night of my life.
Not that I haven't had some stressful moments in WWE. The
difference is, in sports entertainment, if a match or something
else isn't going your way, you can change it immediately.

Election results can't be changed. Enough people voted for
you or they didn't. You either won or you lost. No *Raw* general manager or Vince McMahon is going to come out and hit
the reset button.

Then Bryan had more bad news. Apparently, the county's
website had gone down due to a denial-of-service attack from
a hacker. My only way of getting election results was from
Bryan, who was at the election commission, calling me every
ten minutes.

I was at the campaign's watch party at a hotel, but I spent

most of that time of uncertainty walking around outside. I'm a pacer. When I get nervous, I can't sit.

So there I was, just walking around outside—all night.

This was the big election for me. Knox County leans Republican significantly, so the winner of this primary was favored to beat the Democratic candidate in the general election.

As the results came in, we made steady progress. Slowly, we were adding about fifteen votes per update. I was finally up by about 150 votes, but the last two precincts to report were in the neighborhood where my closest opponent lived! I didn't have a good feeling about that.

Then Bryan called me. "We did it! We did it!" he said.

We *won*!

I won by *twenty-three votes*! This was out of 48,000 votes cast! It doesn't get much closer than that.

When people tell you your vote counts—it really does!

But I couldn't give a victory speech that night. As I was getting the good news from Bryan on the phone, I could hear my supporters inside the hotel cheering. I told everyone that it was too close for the county to call the election. They would still have to count the provisional ballots, which could have been cast by people accused of felonies, anyone with a questionable address, or those with issues that could invalidate their ballots.

After all votes were counted, I had won by twenty-three votes.

As I walked around outside, nervously wondering about the election, I sweated heavily. This was early May in Tennessee, so it was not exactly our cold season. I had to do a number of television and other interviews that night looking like a sweaty mess.

The next day, I flew to New York City for WWE business;

Bryan called me to say Fox News host Neil Cavuto wanted me to appear on his show. There were many media inquiries about the likely "Mayor Kane."

Though I wasn't the first WWE star to take this path, I had known that if I won, people would be fascinated with the wrestler who was getting into politics.

But I had always been interested in politics.

Political Roots

One of my earliest memories as a child involved politics. I was riding in the back seat of the car with Mom and Dad, who were Barry Goldwater conservative Republicans, though politics was not something we discussed much.

As we drove under high-voltage power transmission lines, my mom talked about how horrible eminent domain was. Eminent domain is the right of a government to take private property for public use; it is often invoked when power companies want to get land for their power lines. I always remembered Mom saying that. It stuck with me.

I was a junior in high school in 1984, when President Ronald Reagan was running for reelection against Walter Mondale, the former Democratic senator from Minnesota who had chosen Geraldine Ferraro as the nation's first woman vice presidential candidate for a major political party.

In a mock debate at school, I represented Mondale. Someone asked if I had chosen my VP because she was a woman. I said that I picked her because she was the best candidate for the job.

When I went to college, of course, I was exposed to a lot of the hard left and socialist ideas that are prominent on many American campuses. I listened and considered the many different points of view I heard.

Then I left school and realized that none of that stuff was going to work in the real world!

But it was my years of work as an independent contractor for WWE that contributed most to my fiscal conservatism. As independent contractors, WWE performers are required to keep track of their earnings and pay federal income taxes themselves. That makes you acutely aware of how much you really pay in taxes. To see that money so often wasted or used in ways you disagree with is infuriating.

If I were to become president, my first act would be to work with Congress to repeal the withholding tax. When people get their money back from the government each year, they're not celebrating a rebate. They're getting back the money they overpaid in the first place!

If everyone had to pay taxes themselves—to actually write a check—as WWE Superstars and other independent contractors do, instead of having them automatically deducted from their paychecks, there might be a revolution in this country.

Why Not Run for Mayor?

One day in 2015, I woke up with the idea that I could be mayor of Knox County, Tennessee. The mayor at the time,

Tim Burchett, was stepping down. It's easier to win an open seat than to unseat an incumbent.

The timing was right. At forty-eight, I was getting a little older, and I knew that my full schedule with WWE was not going to last forever. I had always been active in my community, and this would be a way for me to contribute even more.

Mayors probably have the best job in government because they can get things done. Members of Congress represent just one vote among many. Anyone in an executive position, whether mayor, governor, or president, can do things that members of Congress simply cannot do.

When people ask me about my political future and if I might run for the U.S. House or the Senate, I'm like, "No!" In Congress, I would have a bigger megaphone in some ways, but I can make more of a difference as mayor.

Many people don't recognize the importance of state government and what it can accomplish. That fact was another reason I decided to run.

I started planning far in advance. Two years before I announced I would run for mayor, at the Christmas party for the insurance agency Crystal and I were running, I asked Bryan Hair what he would think if I decided to run for mayor of Knox County. Bryan, who was the branch manager at the bank next to our business, said he would ask to be my campaign manager.

That wasn't the answer I was expecting, but it was certainly encouraging.

Crystal was lukewarm about my entering politics. She would support me no matter what I decided to do, but she didn't necessarily want the spotlight.

For me, that was not an issue, given that I had been in the spotlight for twenty-five years. I was used to it!

Still, she had a point. People aren't out to get you in WWE in the way they are in politics. I actually think that's what keeps a lot of good people out of public service, and that's a shame.

Perhaps most important, I had nothing to hide! There's no hidden agenda or ulterior motive with me. What you see is what you get!

While most politicians try to convince voters that they are indeed the person they see on TV, my job was to convince them I wasn't the guy they had seen on TV!

During my campaign, I didn't have to pretend to be sincere or genuine. I told voters I could be with WWE for the rest of my life if I wanted to. I was giving up not only a successful career, but one in which I had achieved nearly unmatched success. I had already been in the public eye for twenty-plus years with no scandals.

It's not hard to campaign when you're honest and just being yourself!

My entire family was supportive throughout, but I also know some of them had to be asking themselves, "What is he doing?"

Is This the End of Kane?

Since I won my election, many have asked if that means I'm retired from WWE. The short answer is no. I hope that I will always be part of WWE. It's been my second family for over half my life.

But today, my job as mayor is my primary responsibility. I'm not going to let anything get in the way of that.

And my life includes other interests as well. I've opened the Jacobs-Prichard Wrestling Academy, along with my friend Tom Prichard, who's trained everyone from The Rock to Kurt Angle. We are already attracting students from around the world to learn their craft in Knox County.

People think the mayor's job is busy, and it can be. But it's *nothing* compared to my old WWE schedule.

Many people don't understand how crazy WWE Superstars' lives are. Every week, I would typically get home on a Tuesday or Wednesday, depending on the TV schedule. If I was lucky enough to return home on Tuesday, I would have only Wednesday to relax and spend time with family. Thursday was consumed with doing laundry, packing, and making reservations.

Friday, I was out the door and away until the following week!

Even when they're home, WWE stars are still working—scheduling, doing media interviews, or handling other, related obligations. Some people watch WWE and think our job consists of just ten minutes a week on television. They couldn't be more mistaken.

So, the truth is, I have slowed down a lot already—since I took my job as mayor! The few times WWE has asked for Kane appearances since I was elected, the company has bent over backward to accommodate my mayoral duties. They have even rented me a private jet! Those aren't cheap.

As long as being mayor is always the top priority, I don't see any reason why I still can't wrestle every once in a while. It's what I've done nearly all my life! My friend Sen. Rand Paul is an ophthalmologist by trade and still performs surgery on occasion, mostly pro bono for charity. But he also does great work in his day job in the Senate.

There's really no reason Kane can't come back from time to time. Pro wrestling is in my blood and always will be. So is my enduring love for Knox County, Tennesse, and its people.

Some people say you can't have it all. Why not?

Isn't this America?

Protecting the American Dream

One of the biggest reasons I ran for mayor is that I have lived the American Dream, benefited greatly from it, and want to do all I can to help protect it. If we fail to preserve it, we will lose something incredibly special; our kids and grandkids will curse us for that loss.

"Freedom is never more than one generation away from extinction," Ronald Reagan once said. That wasn't mere rhetoric, either. It's completely true.

If you can make a difference at a local level, you can be an example of what good governance looks like. That in turn makes a difference in a larger sense as well, which was my plan all along.

Knox County is already a great place. We have values that are important to me. We are generally a fiscally conservative community. The people basically have a live-and-let-live attitude. They don't want things pushed on them. Who does?

Do we need to fix some things? Of course. What locale anywhere on the planet doesn't have its problems? But, when I look around, I see one of the best places in America. I've been around the world and there's nowhere else on this earth I would rather live. If Knox County wasn't a great place, I wouldn't live here!

But I know we can be even better. That's why I asked to be Knox County's mayor.

My American Dream began over three decades ago when a failed football career led me to enter professional wrestling, which ended up making me one of the biggest names in the history of WWE. I continue to live that dream today as the wrestler-turned-politician who many predicted wouldn't win, but did.

There's no limit to what we can accomplish in this country. Our unique freedom means the conventional rules don't apply. I've been a World Champion and a mayor. On paper, there's no way I should be where I am. It doesn't make any sense that I've been able to live the life that I have. It really seems impossible.

But if you have the drive, the desire, and the willingness to overcome adversity, anything is possible.

My American Dream came true for me. Please believe that your American Dream can come true for you, too.

ACKNOWLEDGMENTS

All throughout my life, I've been blessed to be surrounded by good people. I was born to parents who loved their kids, taught us to work hard, and treated everyone with respect and dignity. History books aren't written about people like my parents, but without decent people like them, our world would be much more harsh, angry, and mean-spirited. Thanks, Mom and Dad, for, well, pretty much everything.

The success of my wrestling career would never have been possible without people like Boris Malenko, who literally took me into his home; Dutch Mantel, who gave me my first break in Puerto Rico; Jim Cornette, who brought me into Smoky Mountain Wrestling and groomed me for WWE; and Jim Ross, who helped open the door into WWE and was always one of my biggest advocates. Thank you, gentlemen, for your guidance throughout my early years.

There are too many people within WWE to thank all of them by name. Obviously, thanks, Vince McMahon for giving me chance after chance until I finally got it right. And thanks to Undertaker, without whom there never would have been Kane. From all the wonderful entertainers whom I've had the honor of performing with, to the production crew and cameramen, to the folks who work behind desks in offices around the world, to everyone who makes this wonderful thing called WWE go, thank you!

This book also would also not have been possible without the input, advice, and work of lots of people. Thank you to everyone involved.

Finally, thank you, Crystal, Devan, and Arista. I never tell you enough how much I love you, how proud I am of you, and how thankful I am that you allowed me to join your little family those many years ago.

INDEX

PHOTO CREDITS